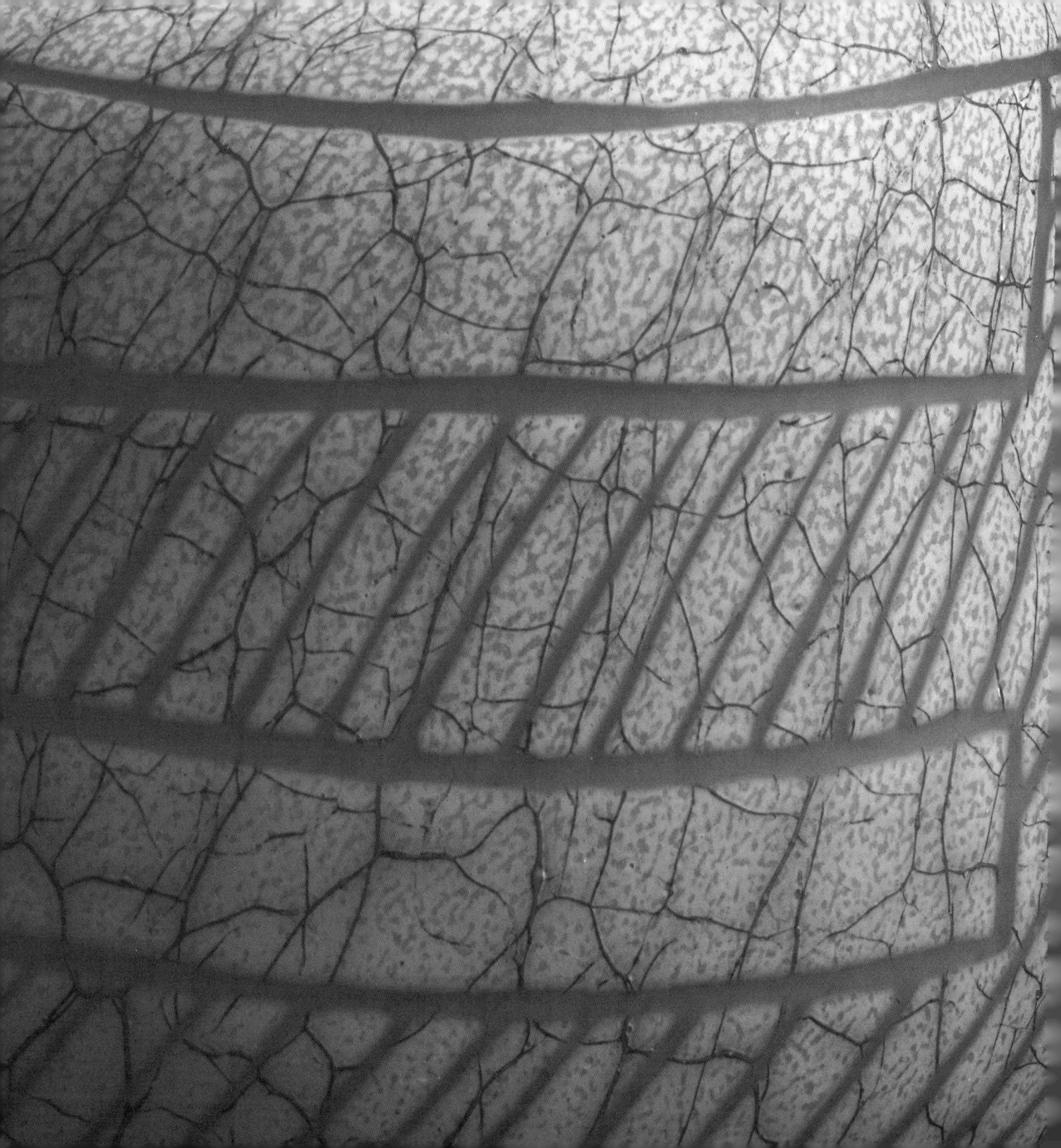

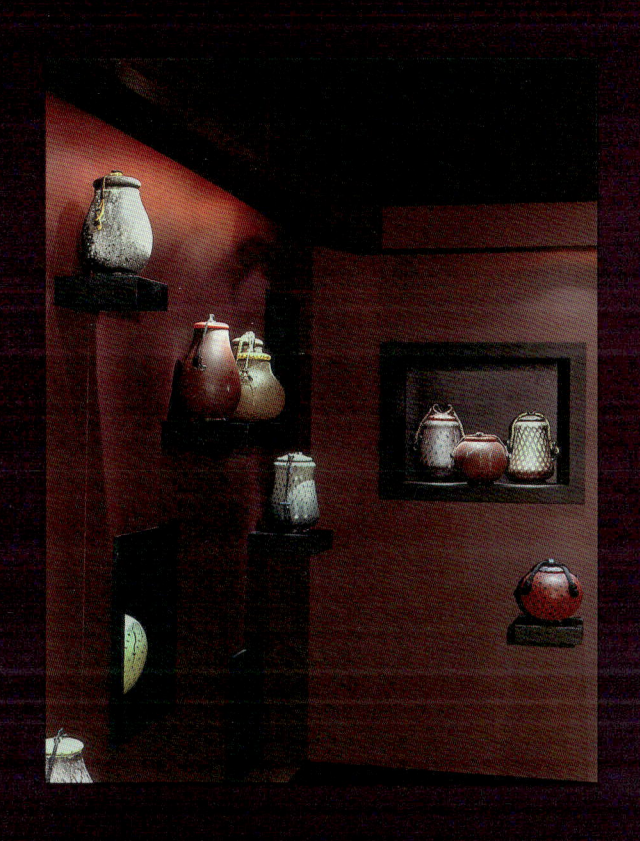

William Morris

CINERARY URN INSTALLATION

Chrysler Museum of Art, Norfolk, Virginia
June 28–August 18, 2002

American Craft Museum, New York
January 17–June 8, 2003

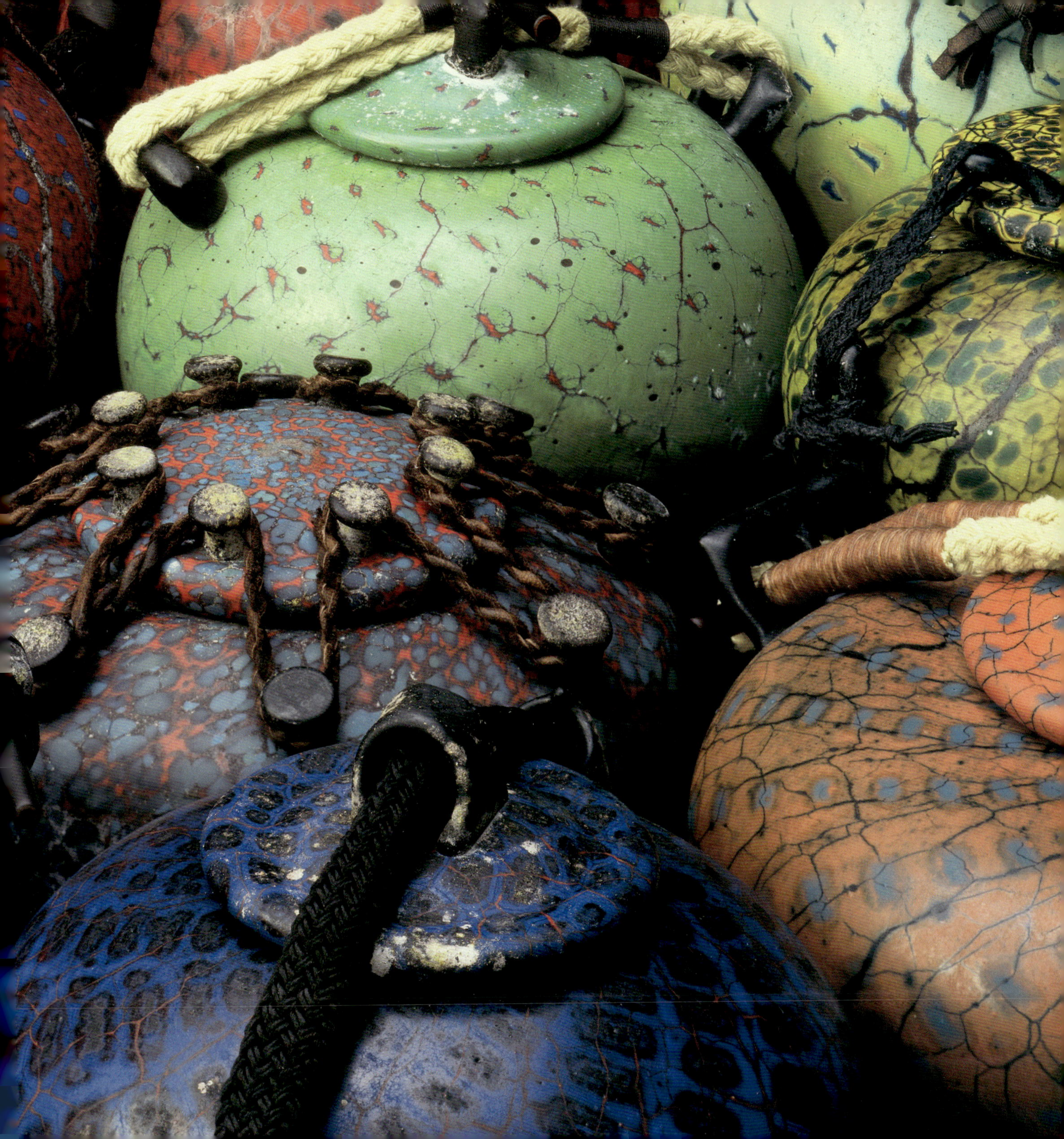

We evade the subject of death until it arrives uninvited, cloaked in an atmosphere of negativity. By nature we are born with the capacity to adapt to transformation, but somehow notions of loss and fear seem to infiltrate our perceptions of this miraculous evolution. However, it is beyond our ideas and thoughts about death that the true mystery and beauty begin.

Our hearts thrive on stories of love and the simple truths they reveal, because some fundamental part of ourselves is confirmed. The *Cinerary Urns* series was prompted by personal experiences with death, beginning with the passing of my mother. Her death was the first in a continuum of seeming tragedies both close to home—with the deaths of friends and mentors—and escalating to include the events of the nation on September 11.

I found myself in a place where my thoughts brought me no solace and my heart could not wander freely because of grim references to mourning and awkward manifestations of grief. The vastness of death as a concept became immediately apparent to me and invited the potential for fear. My mind overruled my heart's desire to dwell in the wonder of the unknown, and I became overwhelmed whenever I attempted to resolve those conflicting feelings.

The first of the *Cinerary Urns* was made for my mother, and it became a focal point for my nomadic thoughts and torrent of emotions. The inspiration was a modest Maasai blood-and-milk jar fashioned from a gourd, with a wooden lid, that I had had in my kitchen for years. I came to realize that by focusing on the urn that held my mother's remains, the object became a springboard from which my mind could rise above the intellect's and the ego's needs for security. The urn was simple in its presence and function; its power was in its ability to become the vehicle through which the realm of the unknown might be accessed. The remains, now dust, reside safely within the jar. It is there that my mind rests and my soul finds its way to the infinite mystery that exists, where it expands into a place of no measure or judgment, no time or concern—to true peace beyond thought.

Even during the process of forming the urns, I tried to develop the shapes in my mind. Never being satisfied with a predetermined notion, I allowed forms to evolve from the realm of the intuitive and was continually amazed by the outcome. A language developed out of this process where the mind did not reign and the heart and soul moved freely.

Mystery is the hidden companion of joy and of loss, both of which are deeply felt but not always understood. We think we know these fundamental emotions until we try to summon them; only later do we realize they are not something we can control. The feelings arrive unannounced, and we must be willing to recognize and embrace them fully. Our creativity and intuition access endless magic. If we draw upon them during the mourning process, many of our learned notions about death—taught to us so that we might be spared pain and discomfort—dissolve, bringing us to a place of liquid contemplation. As a Shoshone medicine man questioned, "If the dead be truly dead, why should they still be walking in my heart?"

WILLIAM MORRIS

6

11
September
2001

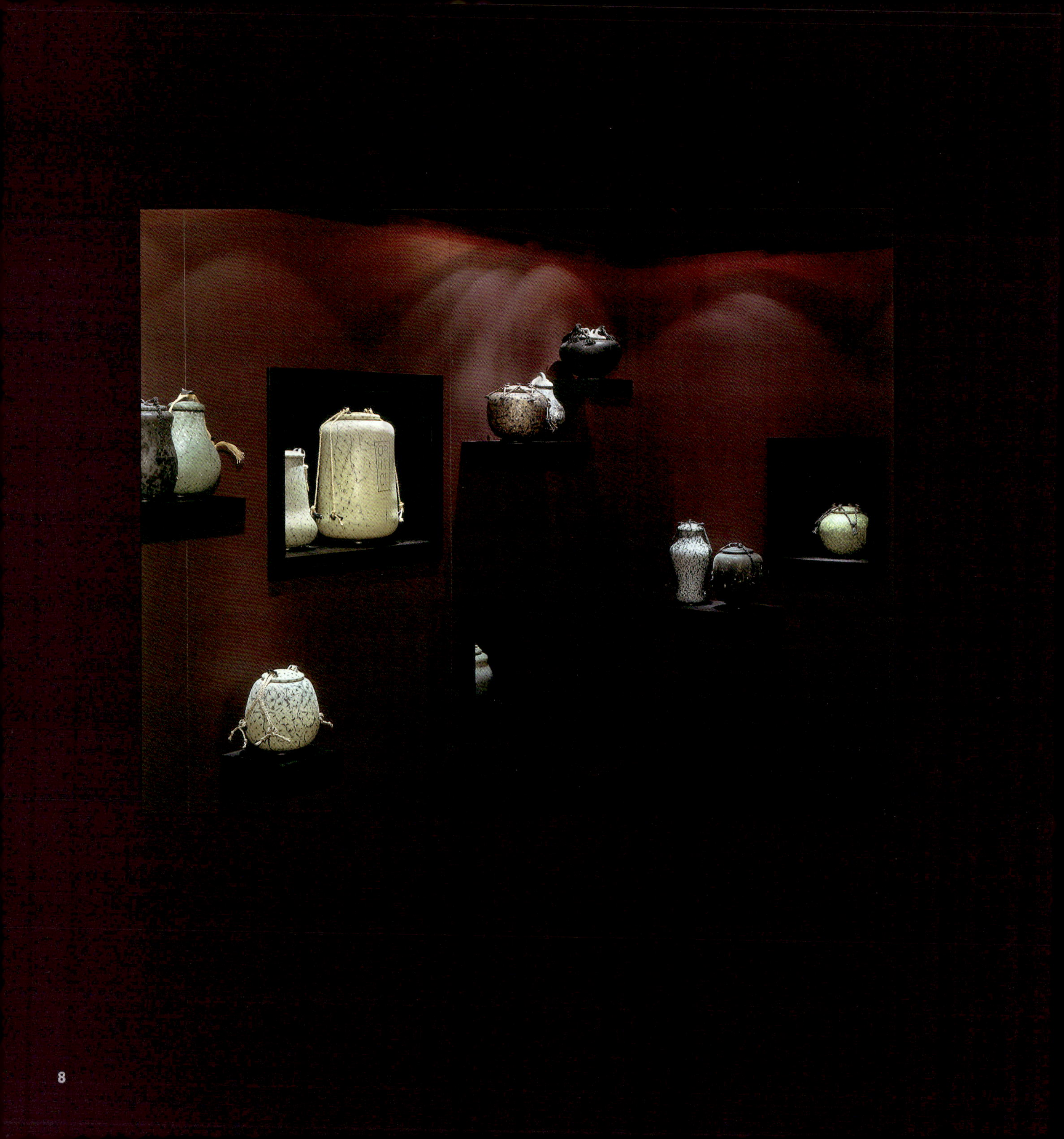

We at the Chrysler Museum of Art, under the auspices of the Chrysler's Masterpiece Society, are proud to premiere William Morris's *Cinerary Urns*. William Morris is no stranger to the Chrysler. He has been represented in the permanent collection since 1995, and in 1999 the Chrysler premiered his installation *Myth, Object, and the Animal* as a key component in the region-wide exhibition *Art of Glass*. The Masterpiece Society, which normally focuses on great painters of the past such as El Greco, Rembrandt, and Monet, has only once before shown the work of a living artist. Interestingly, that artist—Dale Chihuly—also works in glass.

Cinerary Urns is at once a requiem in glass for the victims of the September 11 terrorist attack on the United States and a memento mori for our time. William Morris has been wrestling with imagery of life and death for much of his artistic career and in so doing imbues his glass sculpture with a sense of the spiritual. He has found beauty in decay. Bones, fashioned from glass, have formed a significant element of his artistic vocabulary, symbolizing not only death but also the cycle of life. He has produced fully articulated human skeletons and freestanding groupings of bones and antlers.

Morris first created vessels as containers for remains in the *Burial Urn* series. In the *Canopic Jar* series he carried this idea a step further by enclosing the imagined remains in a jar with an animal-head cover. Ironically, Morris's first essays in the vessel form—*Vessels with Shard Drawings, Stone Vessels*, and *Standing Stones*—were purely decorative. In *Cinerary Urns*, he has come full circle, creating exquisitely beautiful vessels that individually give no outward hint of the sacred function for which the artist ultimately intends them—to hold actual cremated human remains. Grouped in niches as an installation, the currently empty cinerary urns are a powerful vehicle for the contemplation of national and personal grief; yet they are life affirming. The stunning visual effect of the vibrant colors and elegant braided fiber ties calls to mind a verse from Psalm 30 of the Bible:

Thou has turned my mourning into dancing;
thou has loosed my sack cloth and
girded me with gladness.

GARY E. BAKER, CURATOR OF GLASS
THE CHRYSLER MUSEUM OF ART

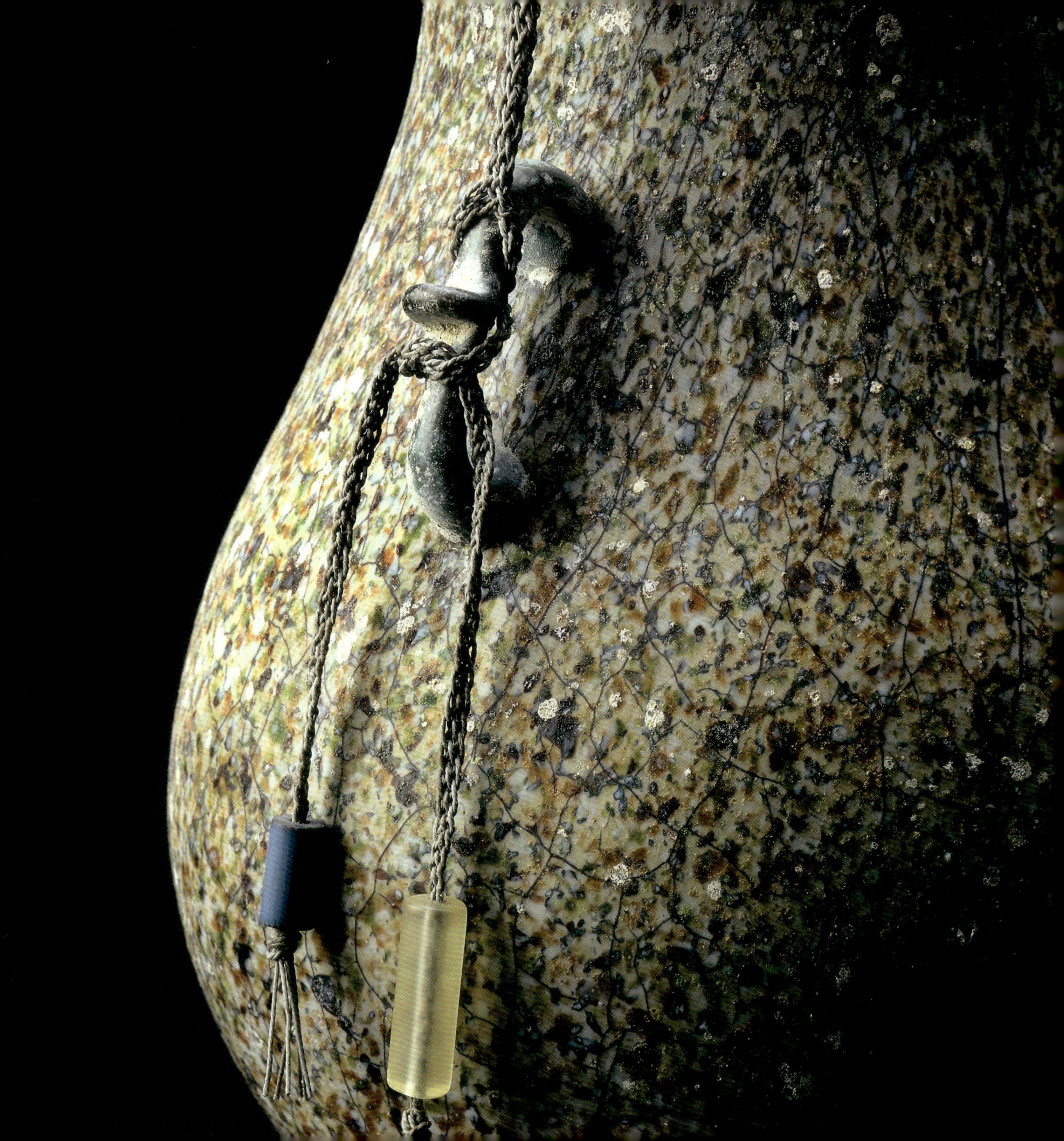

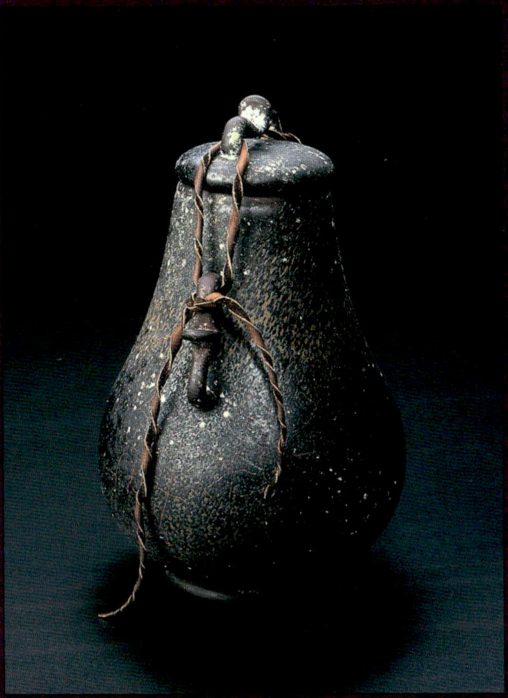
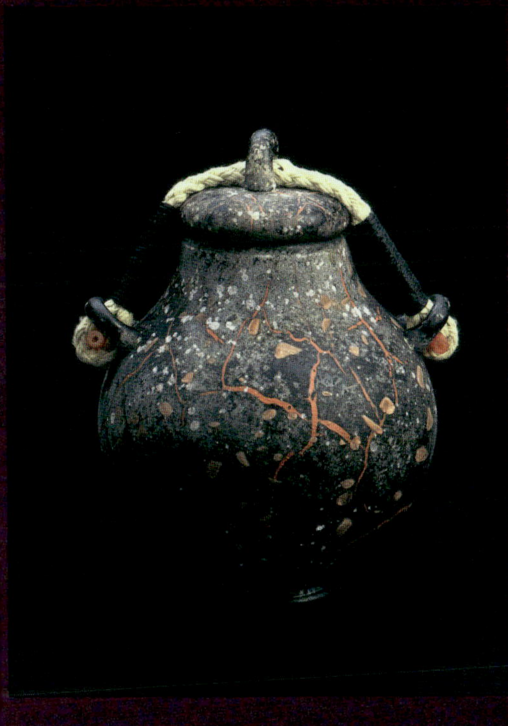
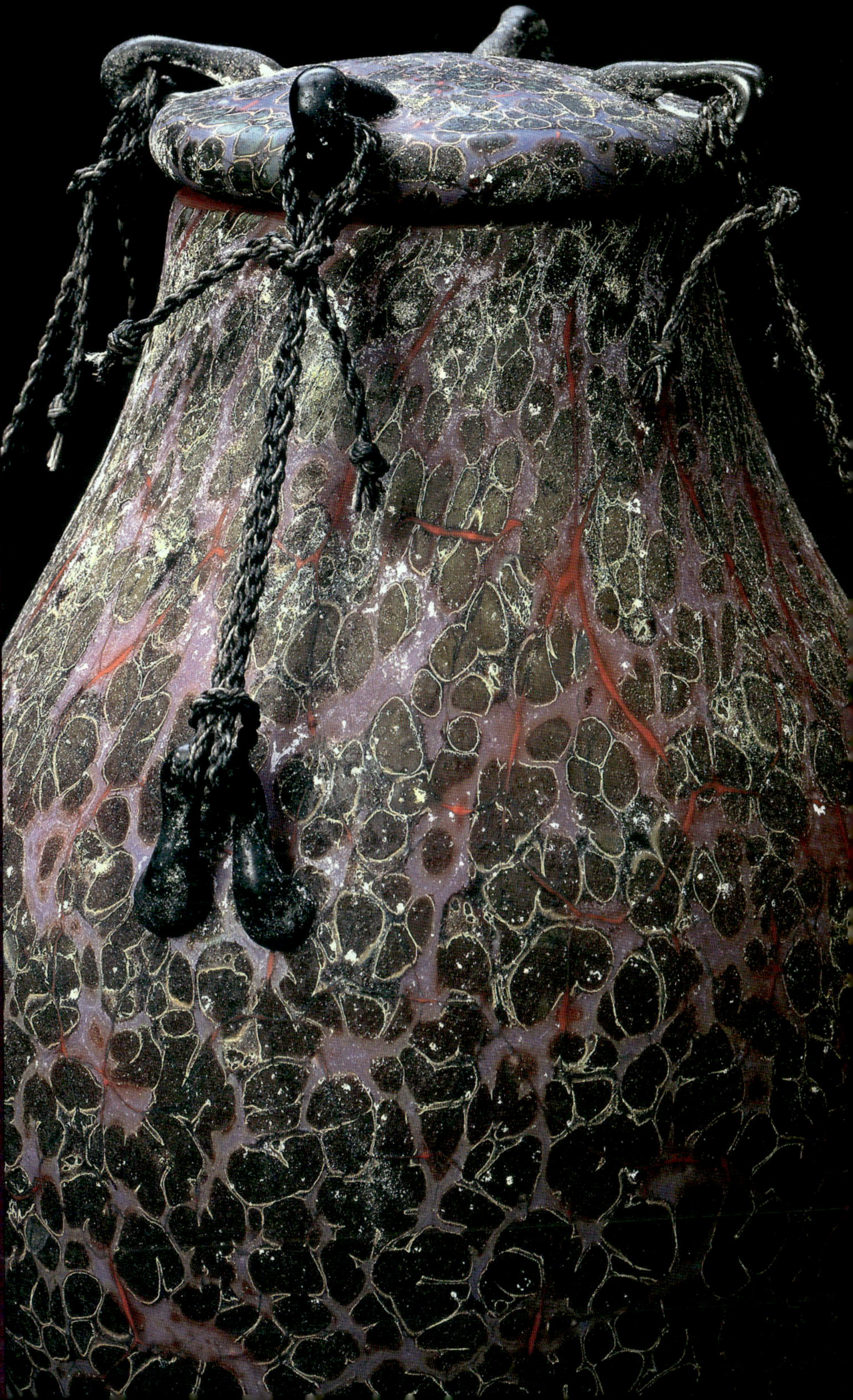

12

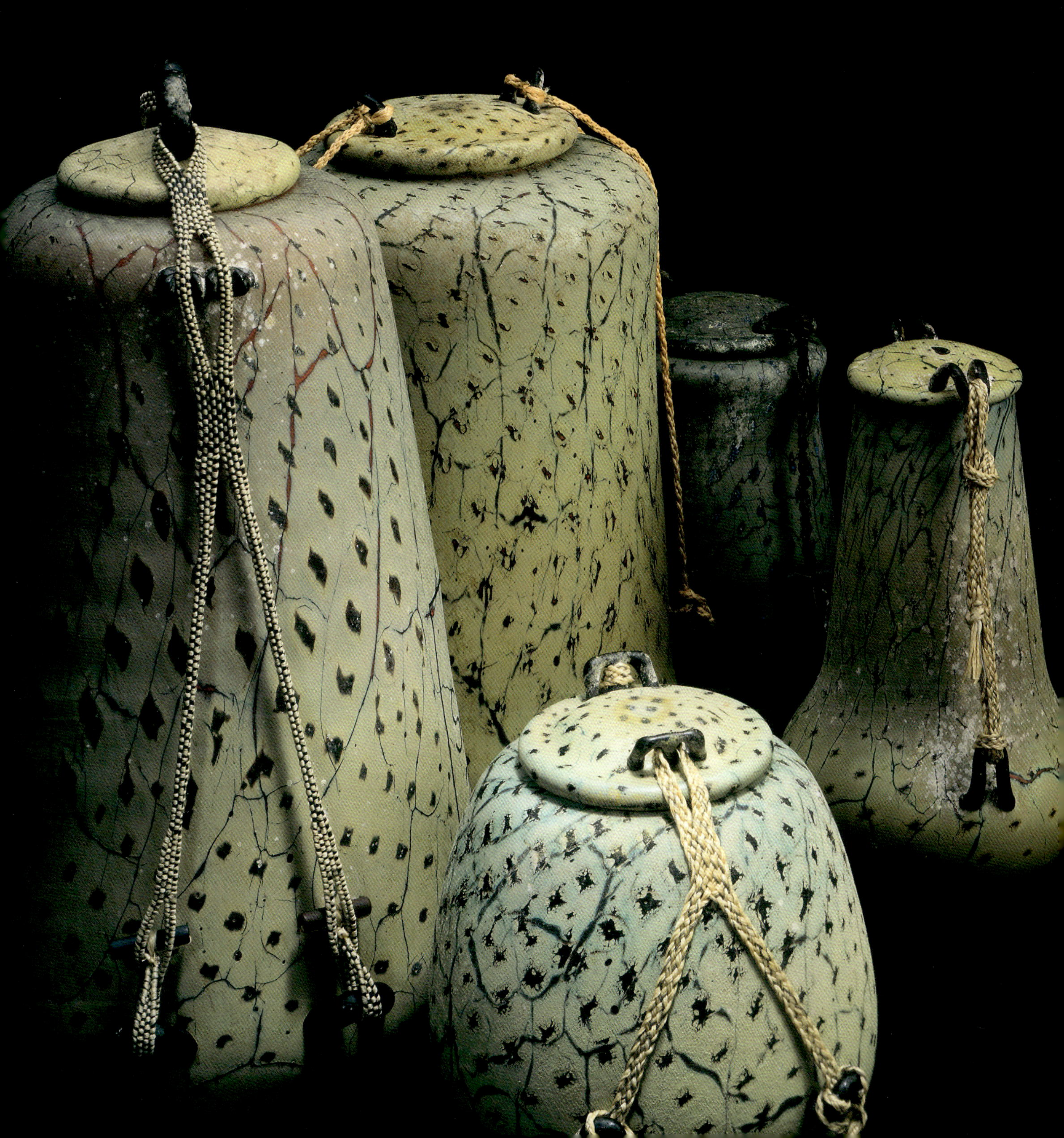

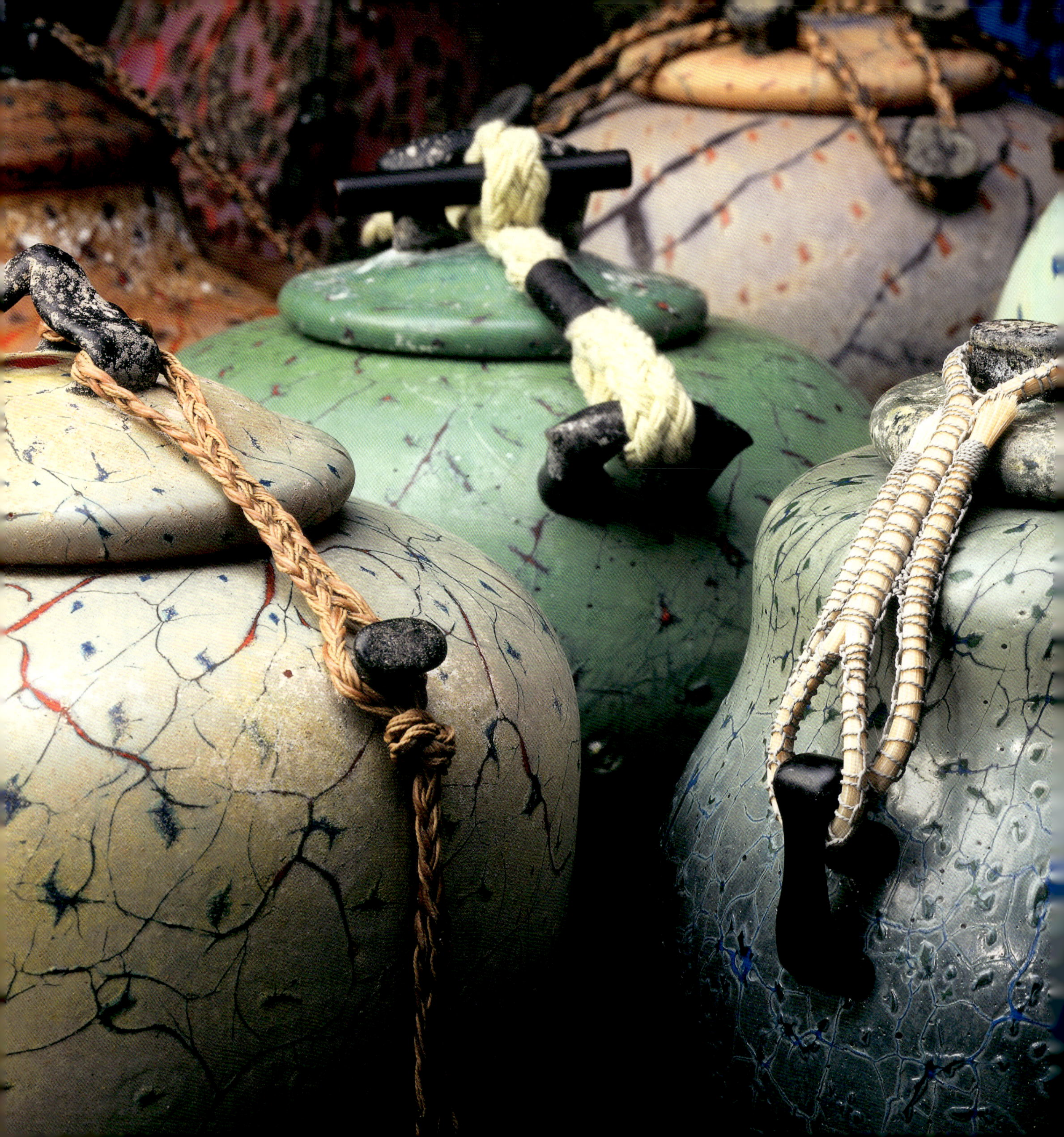

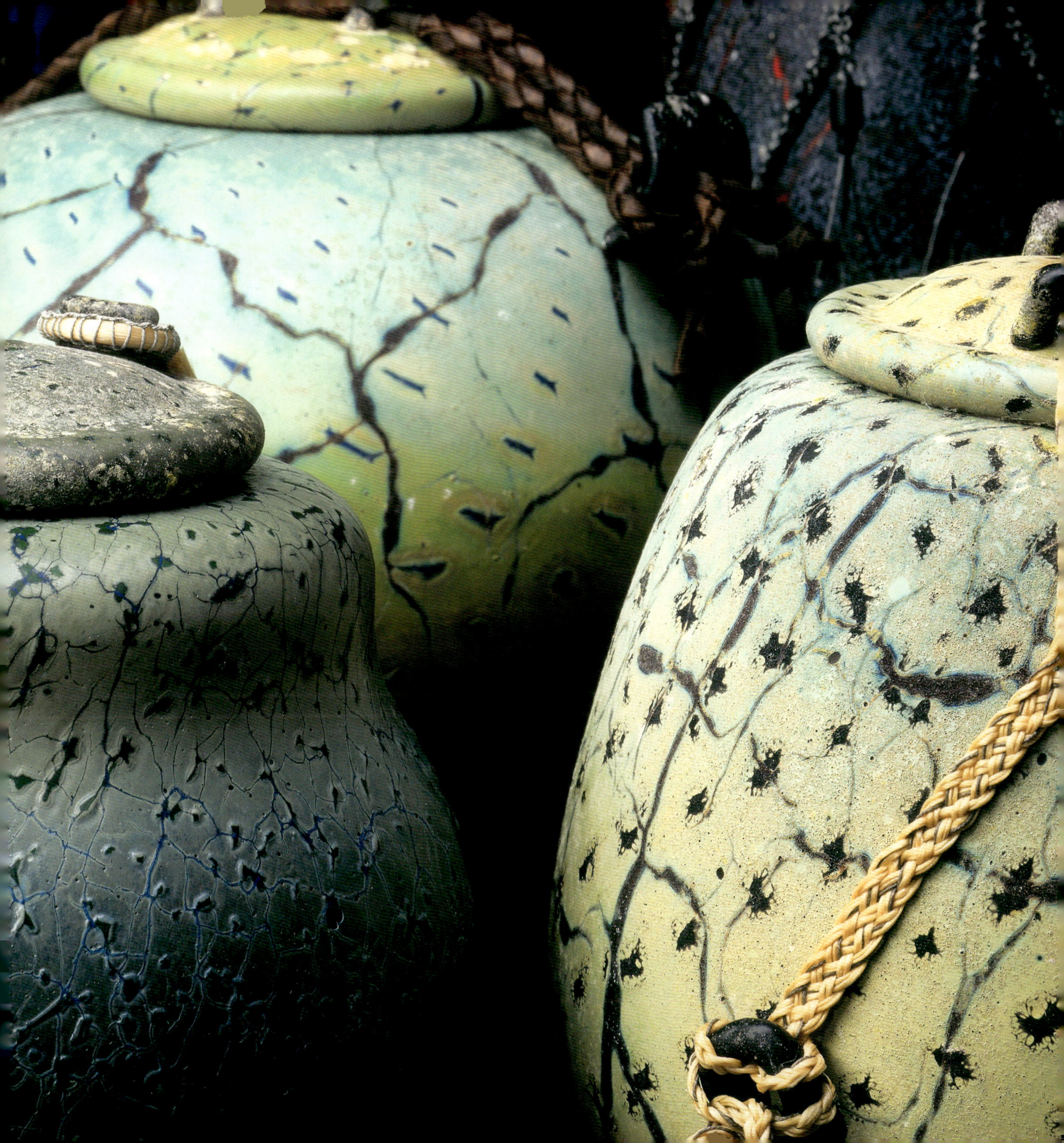

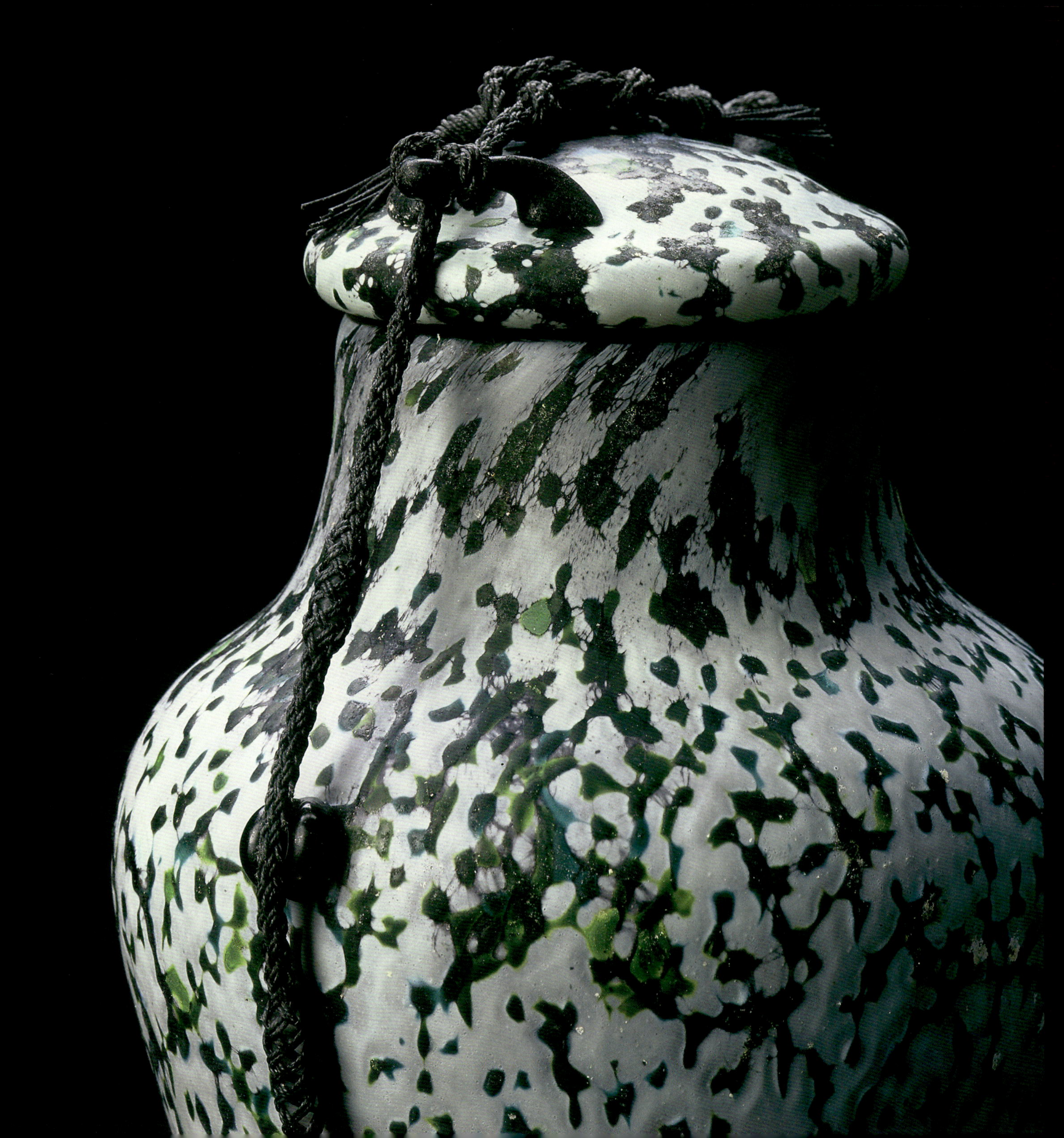

17

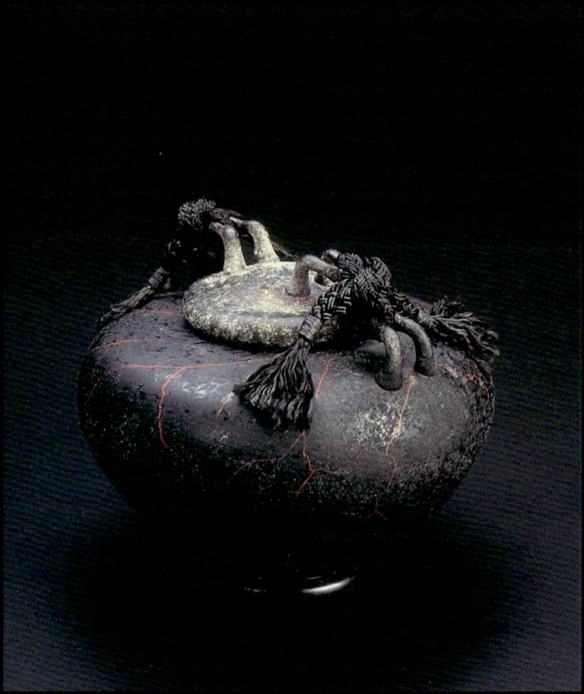

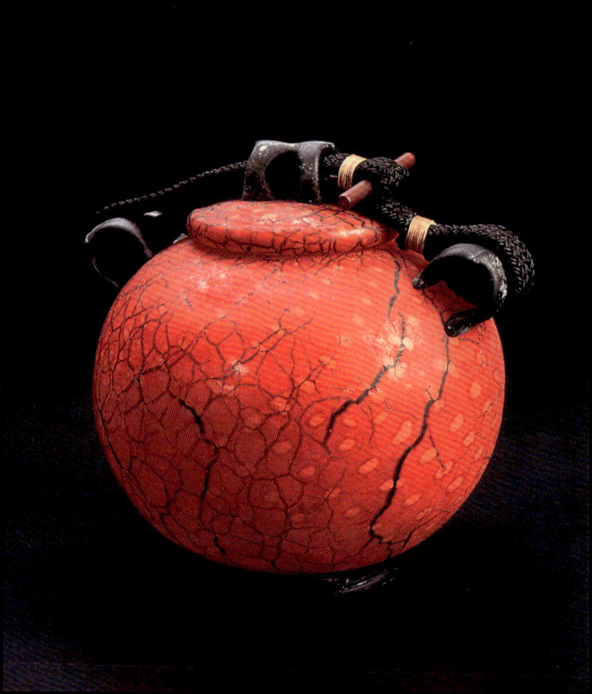

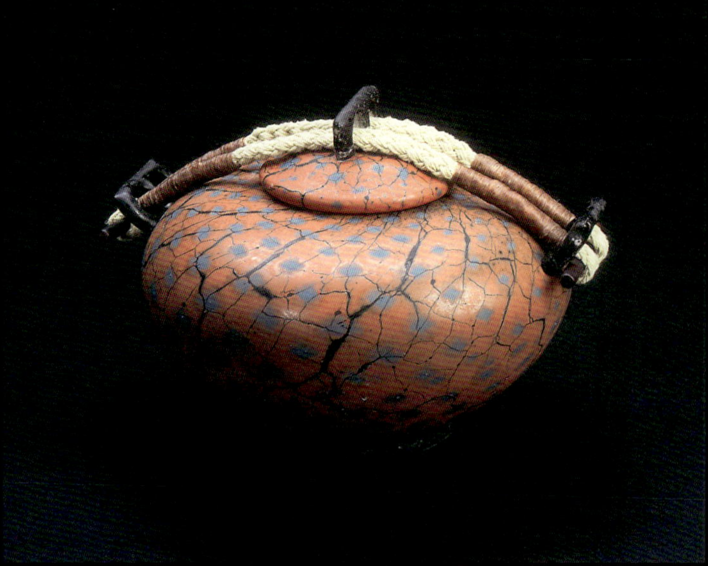

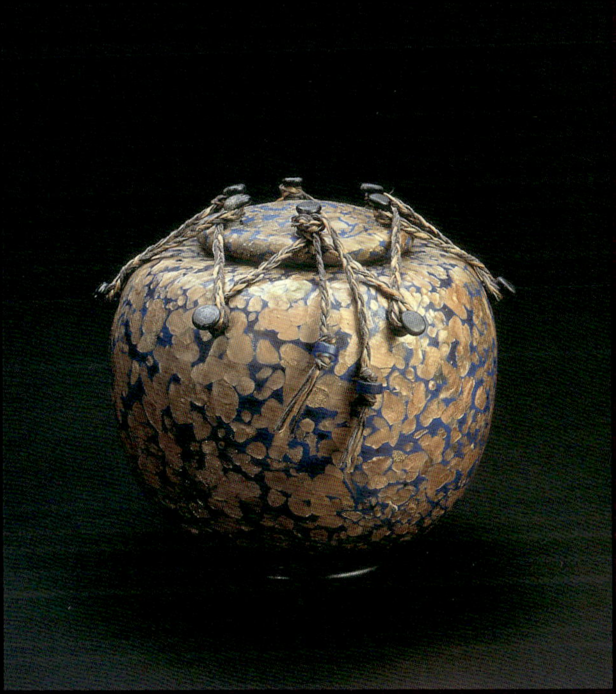

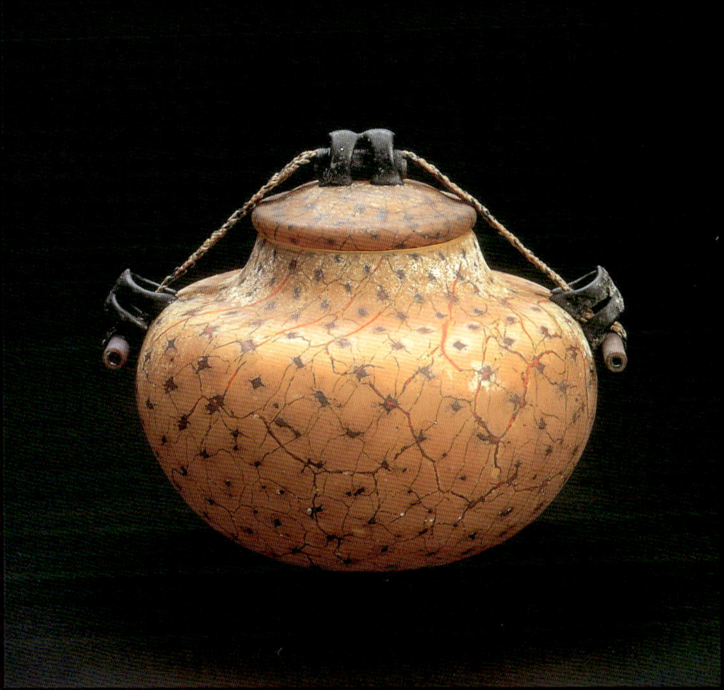

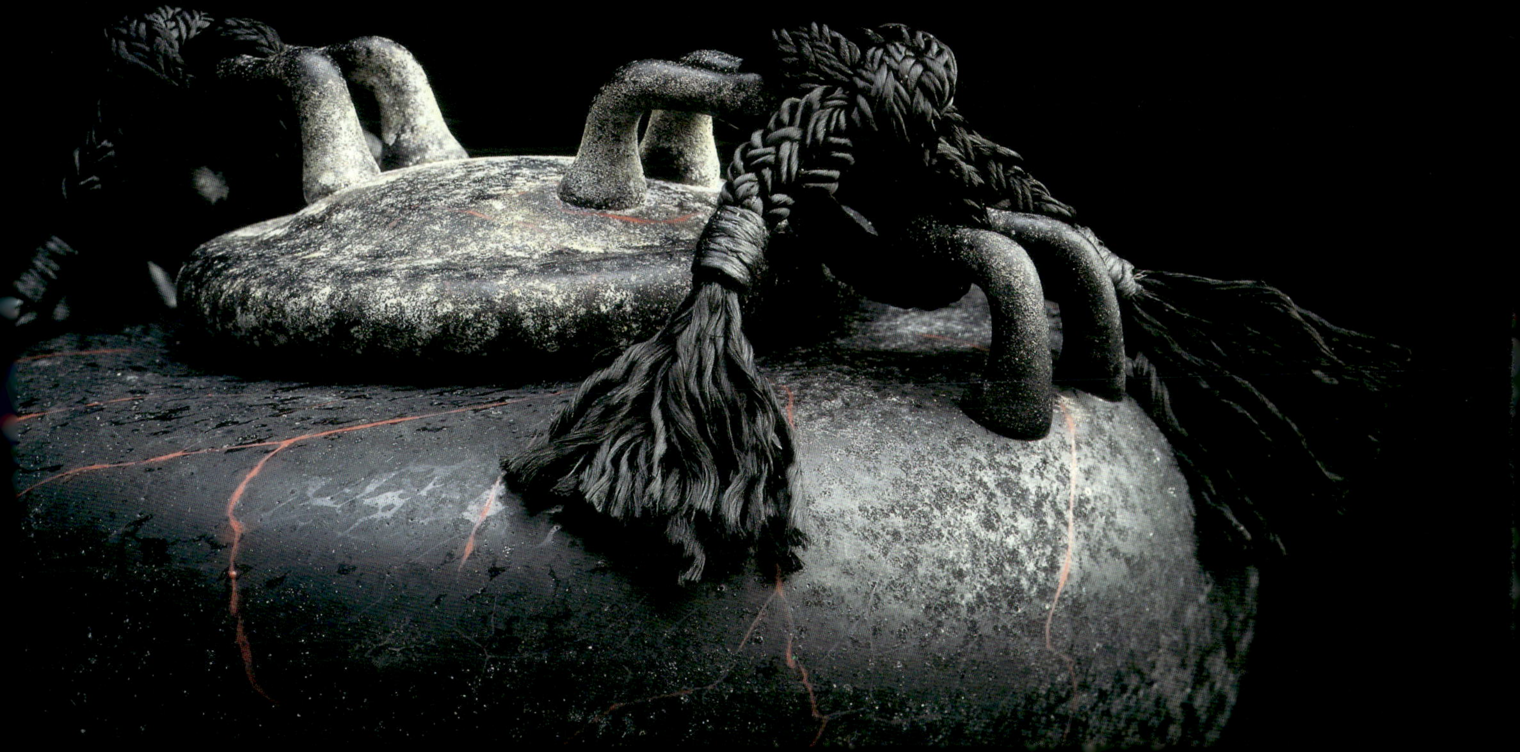

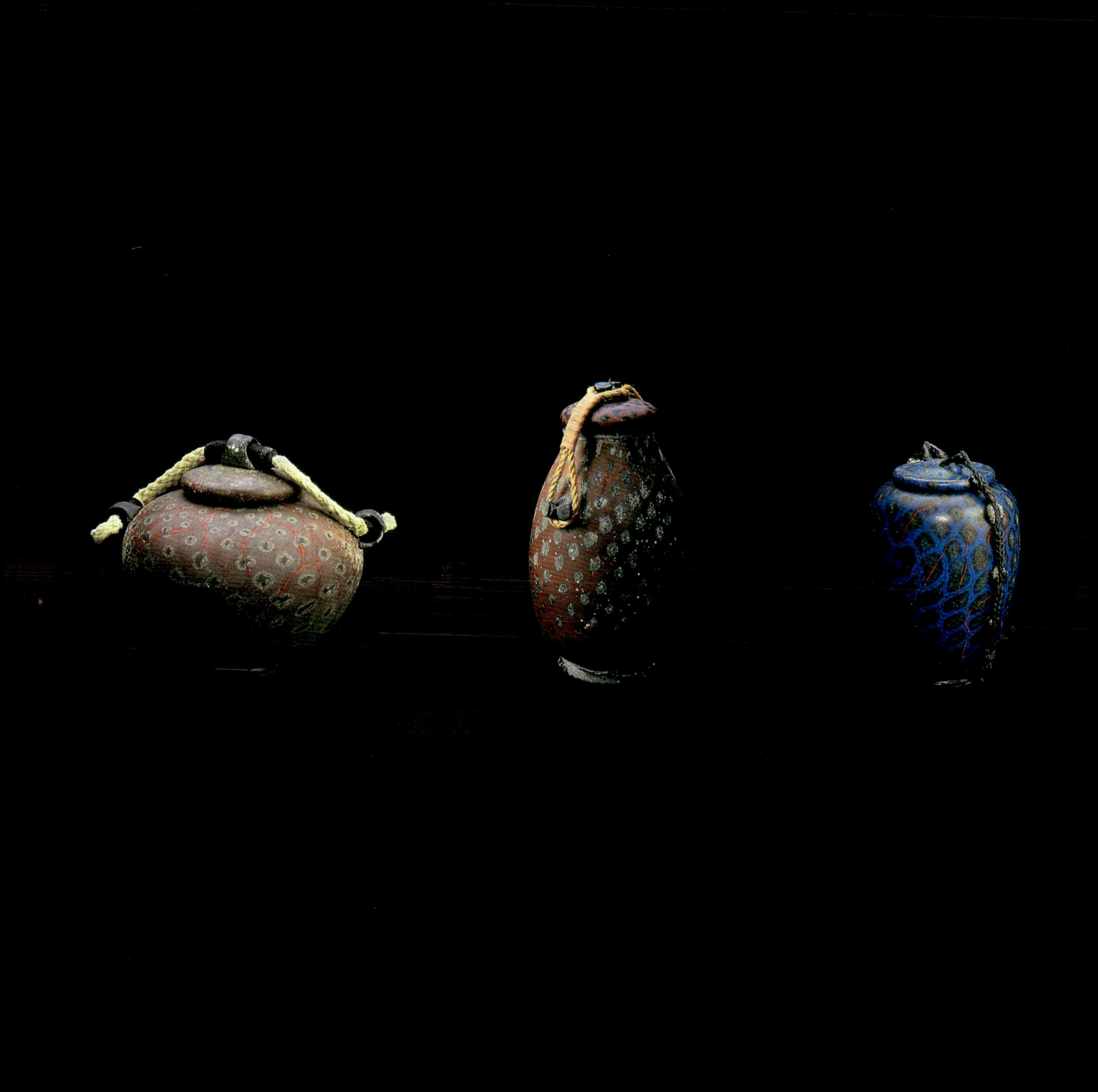

21

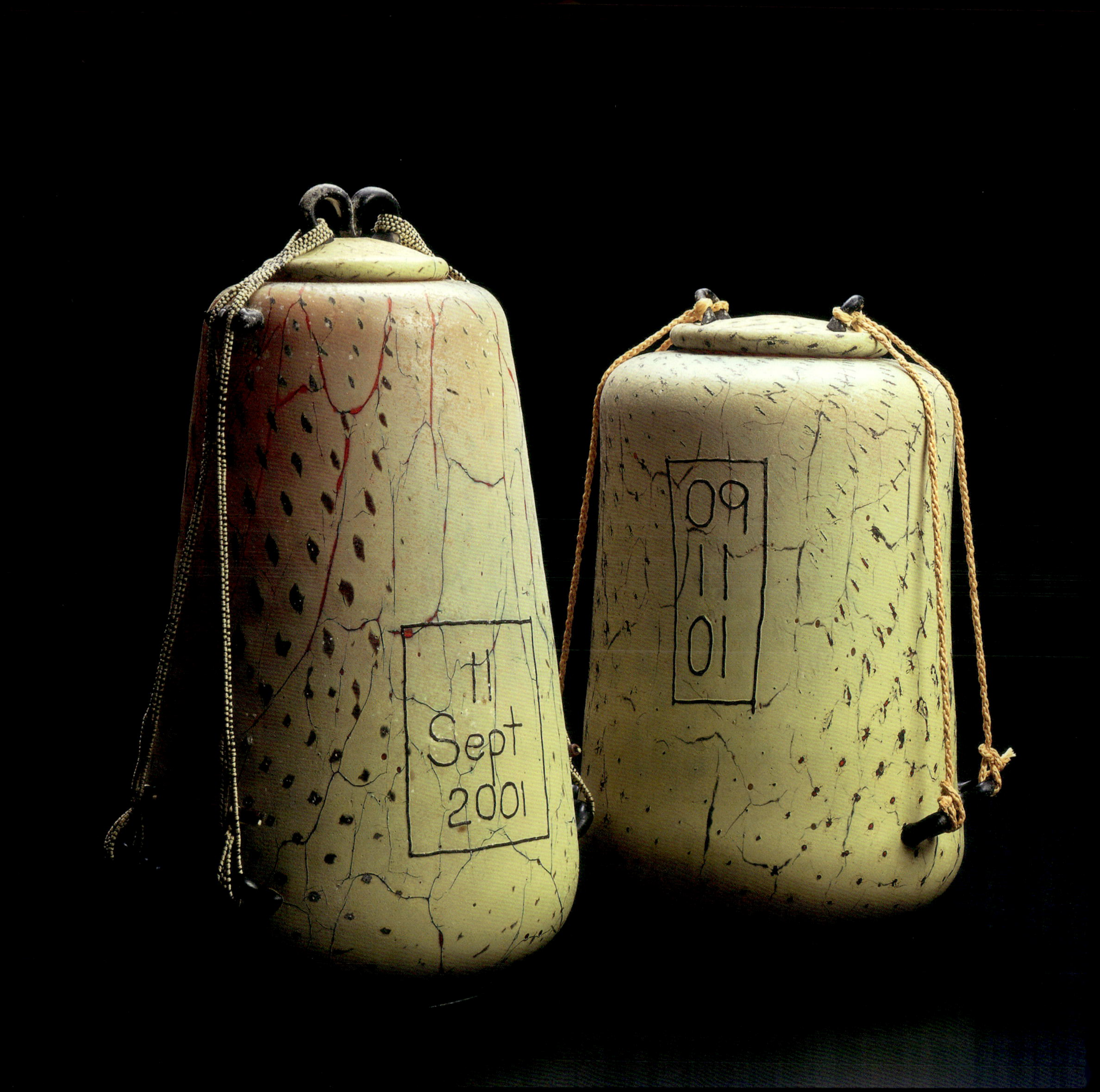
11
Sept
2001
09
11
01

In his thoughtful and moving artist's statement about his cinerary urns, William Morris reminds us that "mystery is the hidden companion of joy and of loss, both of which are deeply felt but not always understood." On the other hand, artists have uniquely understood the power of works of art to embody the most private and poignant intricacies of our lives and spirits. Objects created by artists in any medium, whether it be glass, clay, fiber, wood, or metal, become homes for our longings, our visions, and our dreams. The majority of the objects that remain as documents of any period or culture are those that celebrate or preserve memories, rituals, and events, ranging from birth to marriage to death. Our life cycles as a species are commemorated in objects, and our cultures are transmitted by them from one generation to the next.

William Morris's series of urns speaks to our shared experiences as individuals living in the 21st century, and with particular significance to those of us living in New York City. At the same time, through these simple yet monumental forms, the artist builds bridges between who we are and who we have been. Morris's urns evoke the presence of history and the timelessness of the human spirit. They are at the same moment documents that have special meaning in a time of uncertainty, loss, and sadness. Like the experience of the Greek theater, Morris's installation of cinerary urns offers both meditation and catharsis. In their sheer physical beauty, the urns engage our sense of wonder and our love of color and texture. As embodiments of the ephemeral in the eternal, they are tangible poems of the spirit.

Over the course of its fifty-year history, the American Craft Museum has underscored its belief that the finest creative efforts of artists encourage the finest and most humanistic responses in all of us. The American Craft Museum is proud and honored to share this special experience with our visitors, and we are grateful to the artist for sharing his life and work.

HOLLY HOTCHNER, DIRECTOR
AMERICAN CRAFT MUSEUM

24

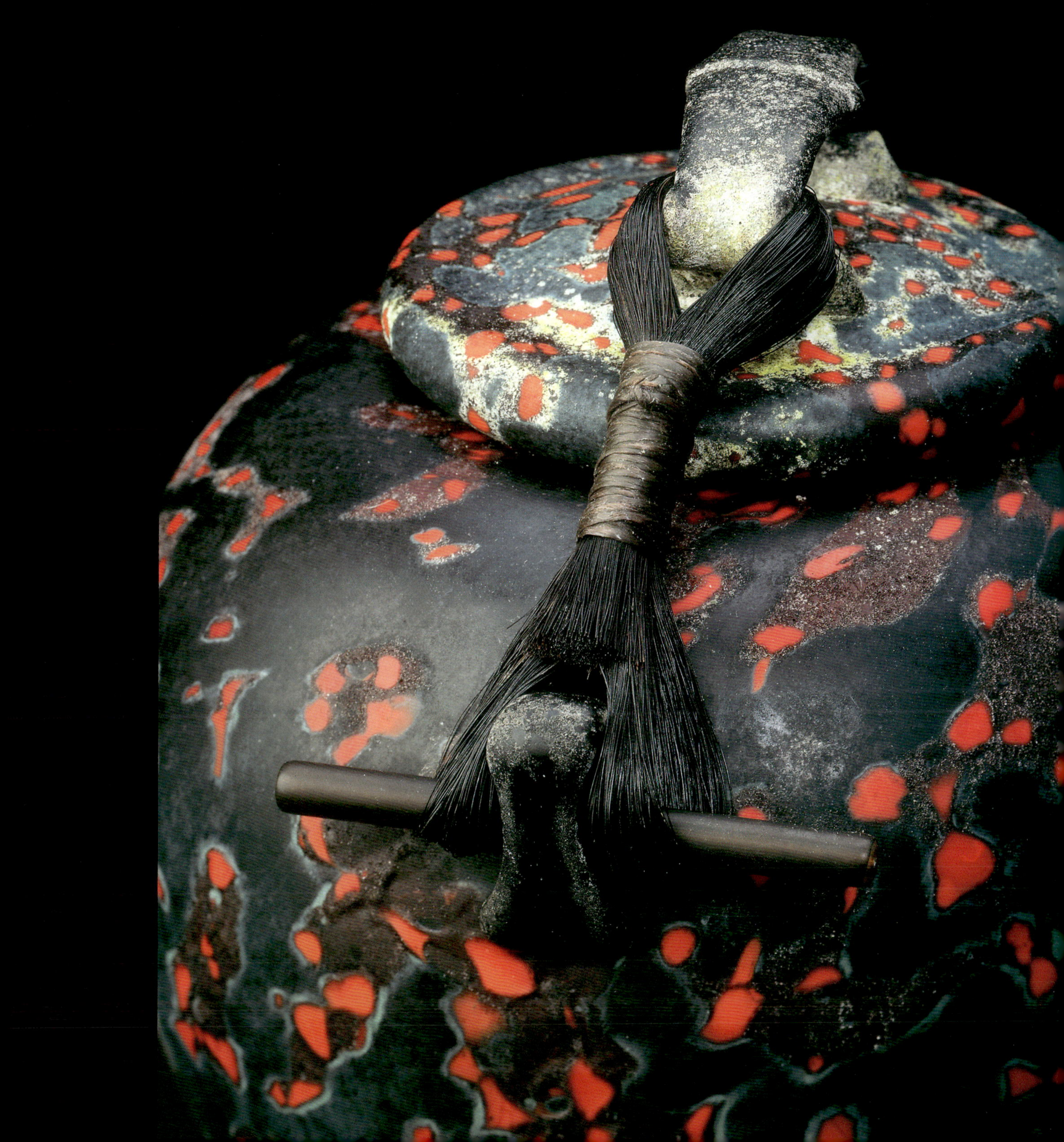

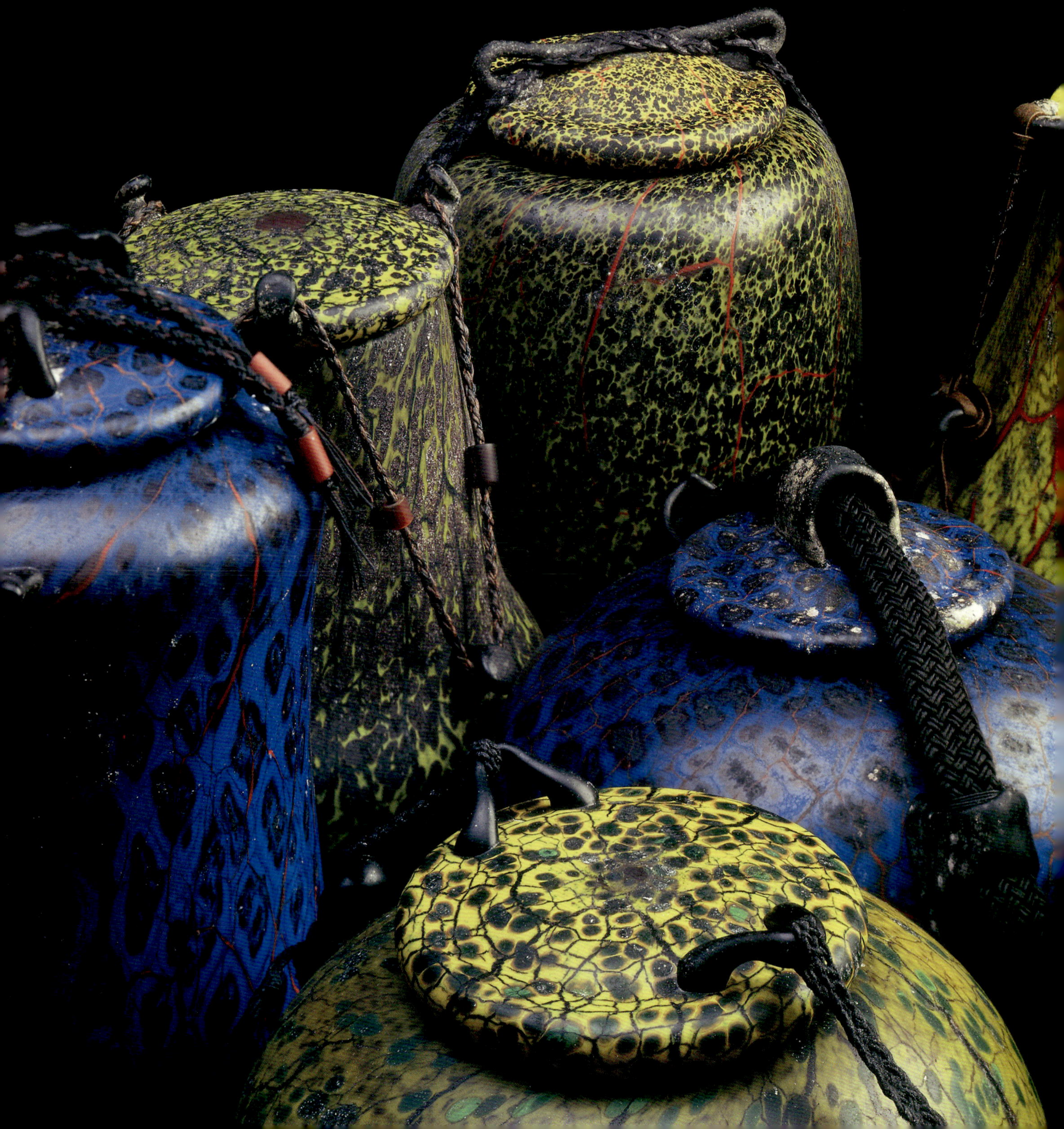

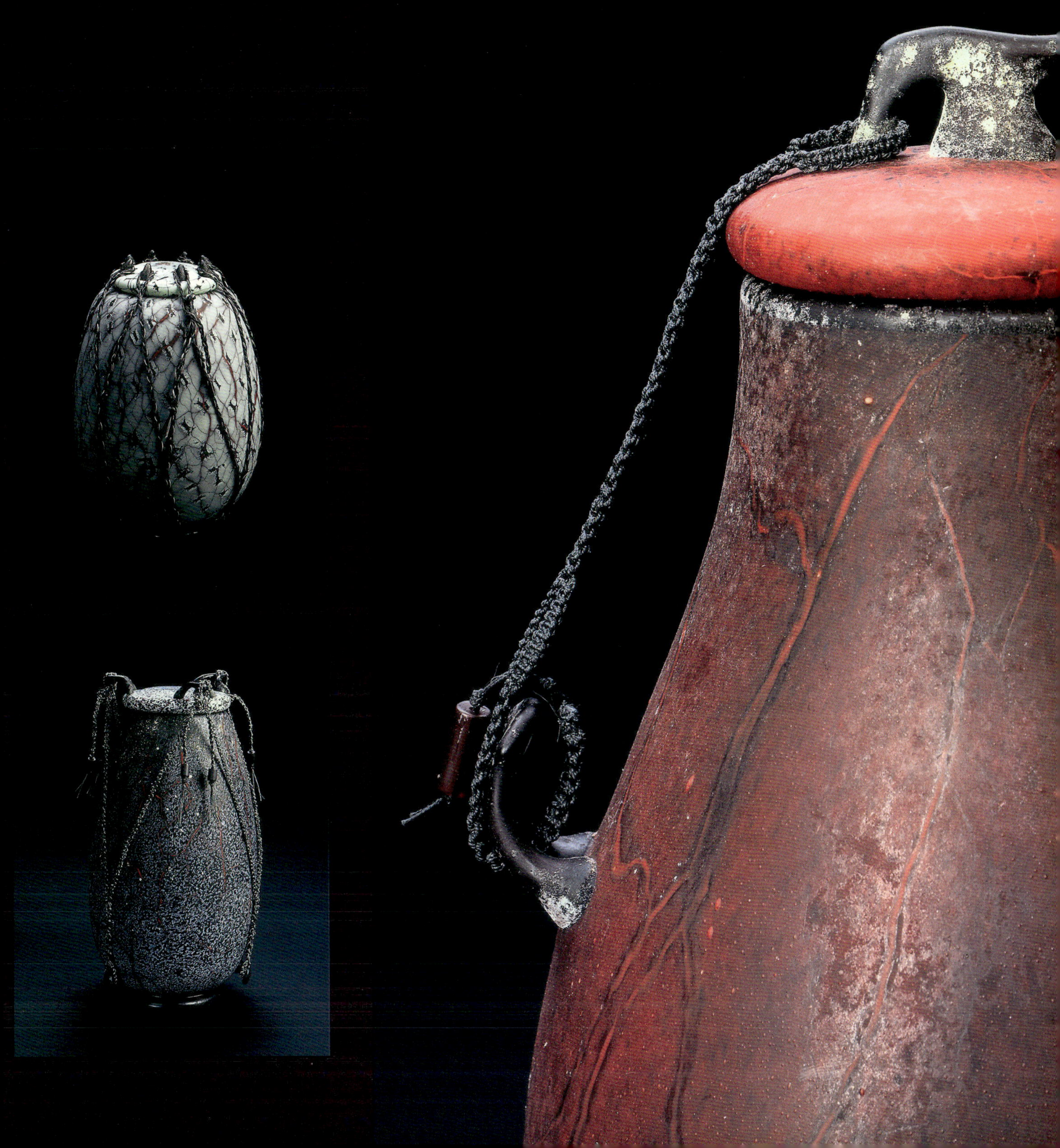

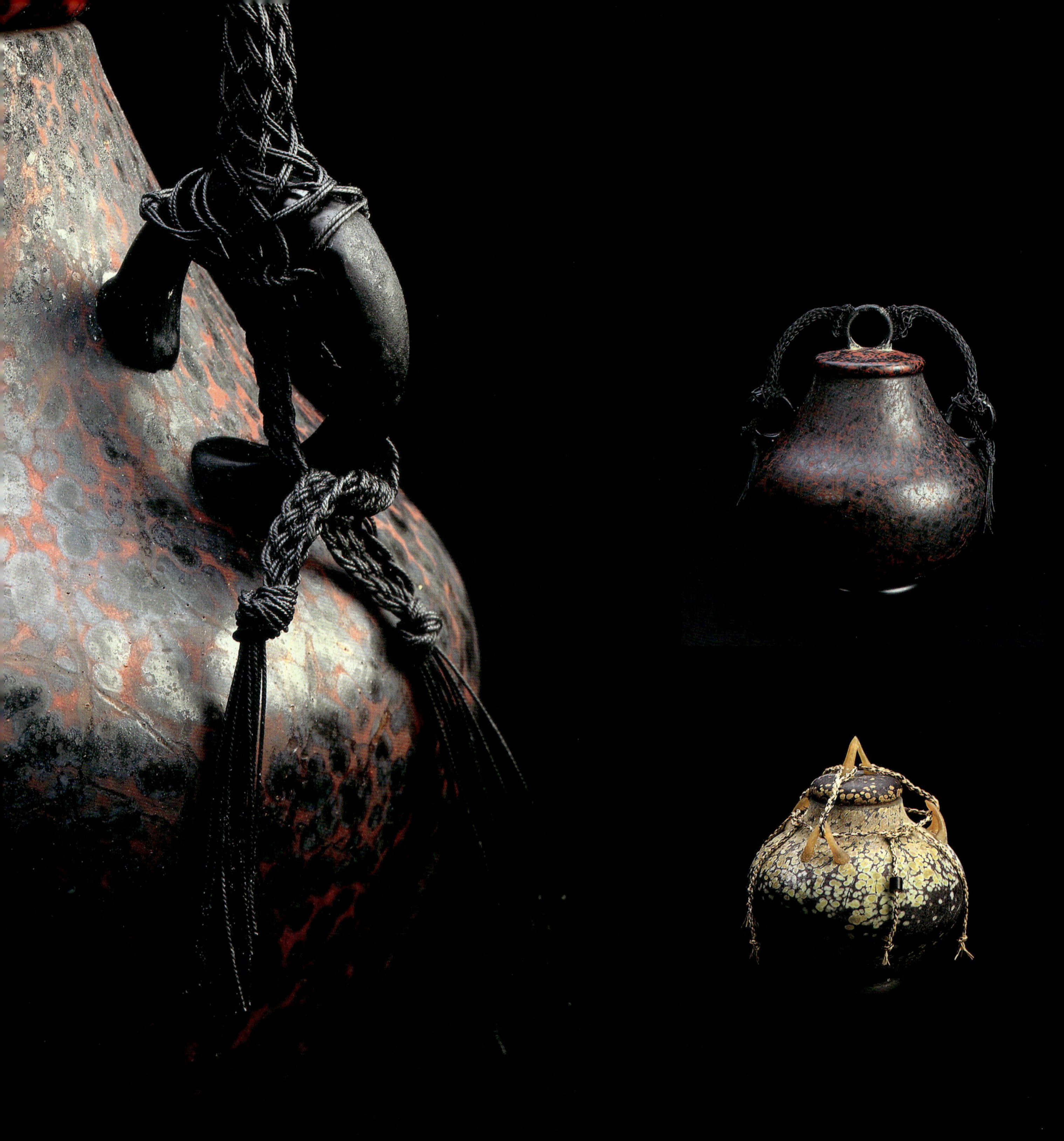

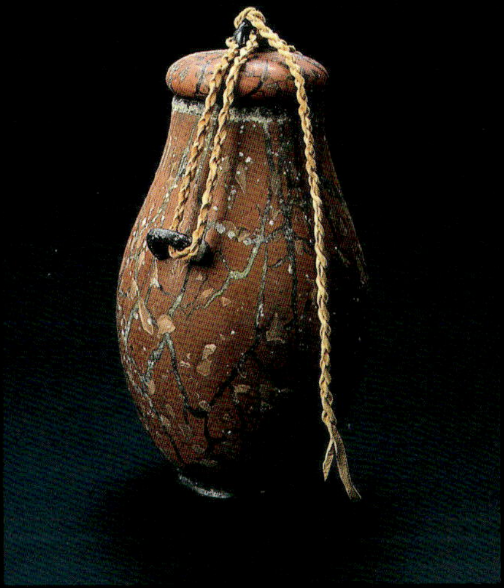
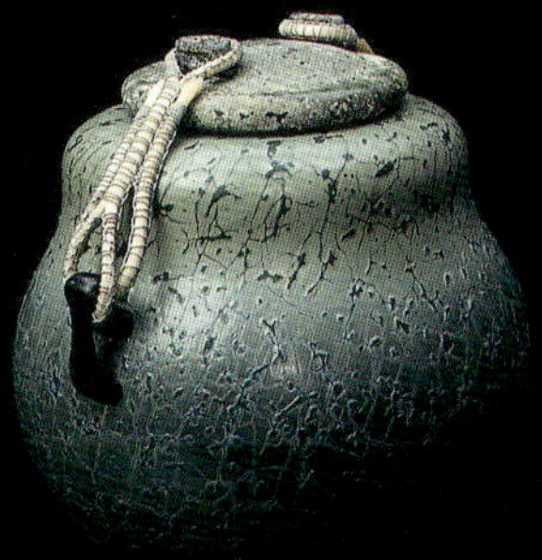
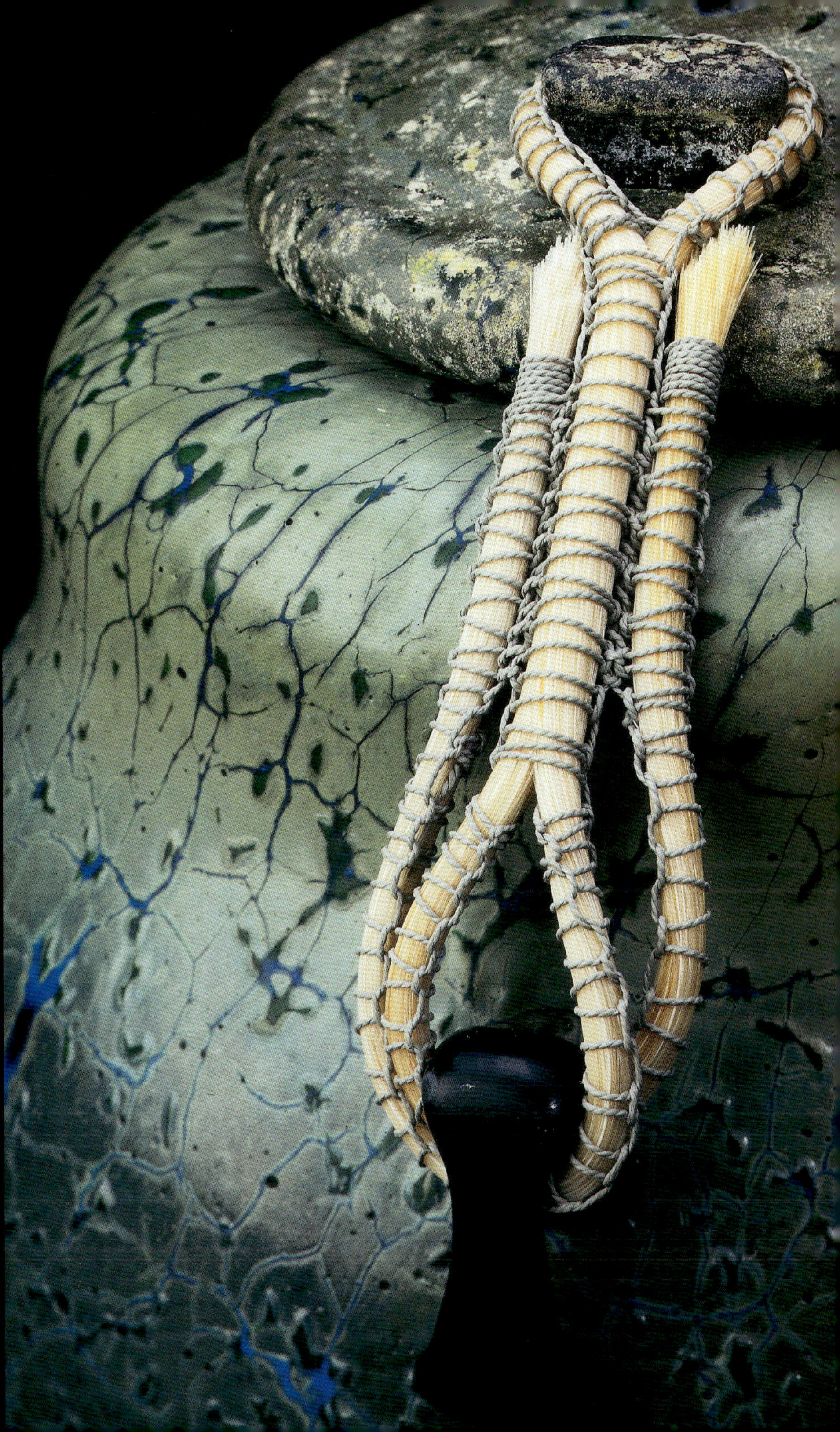

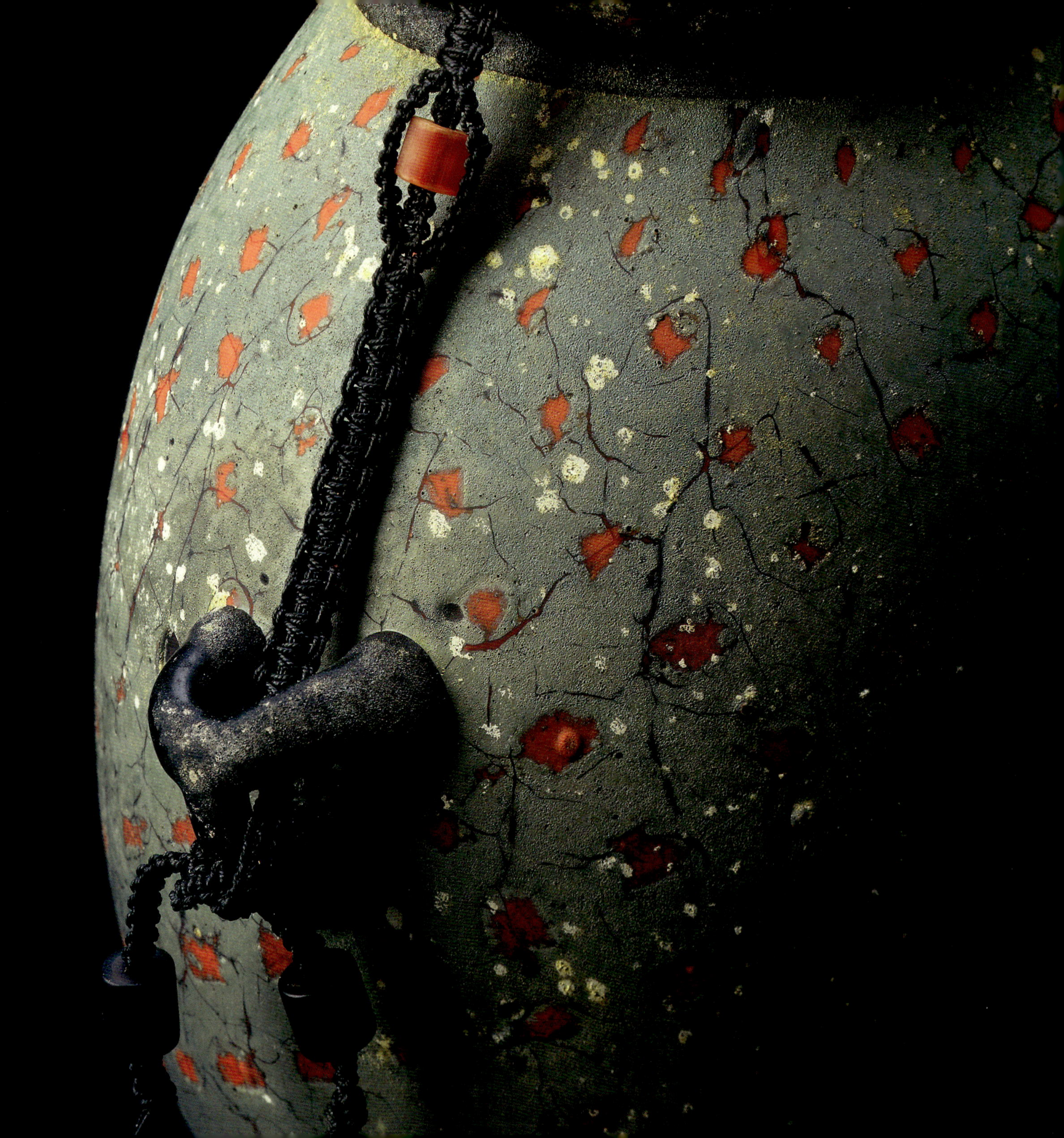

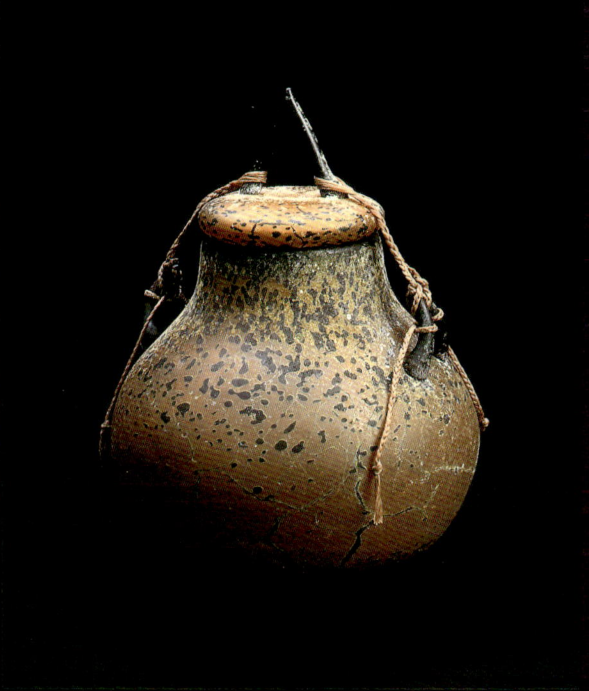

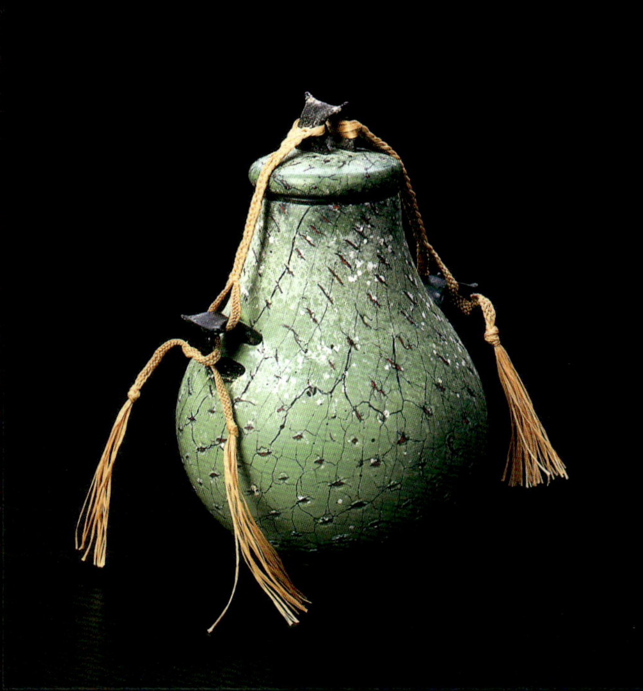

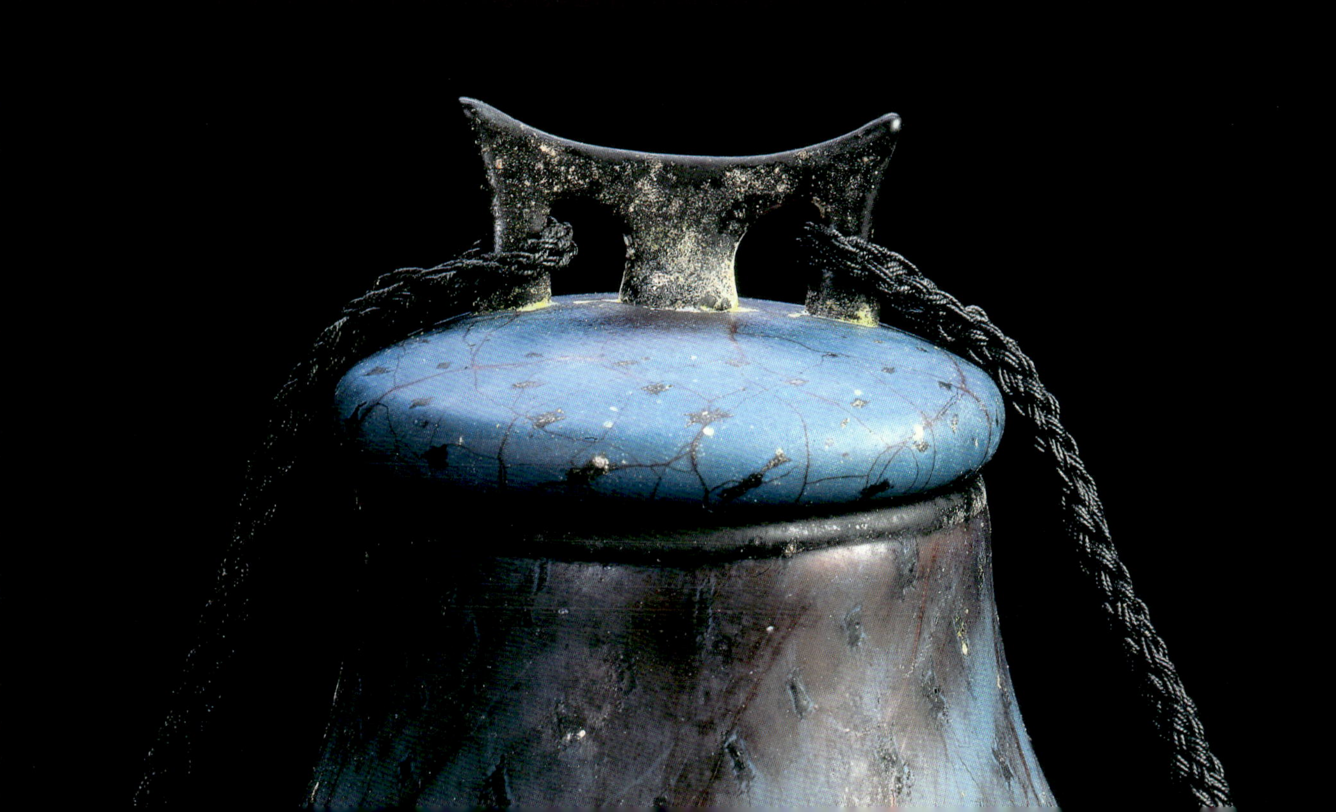

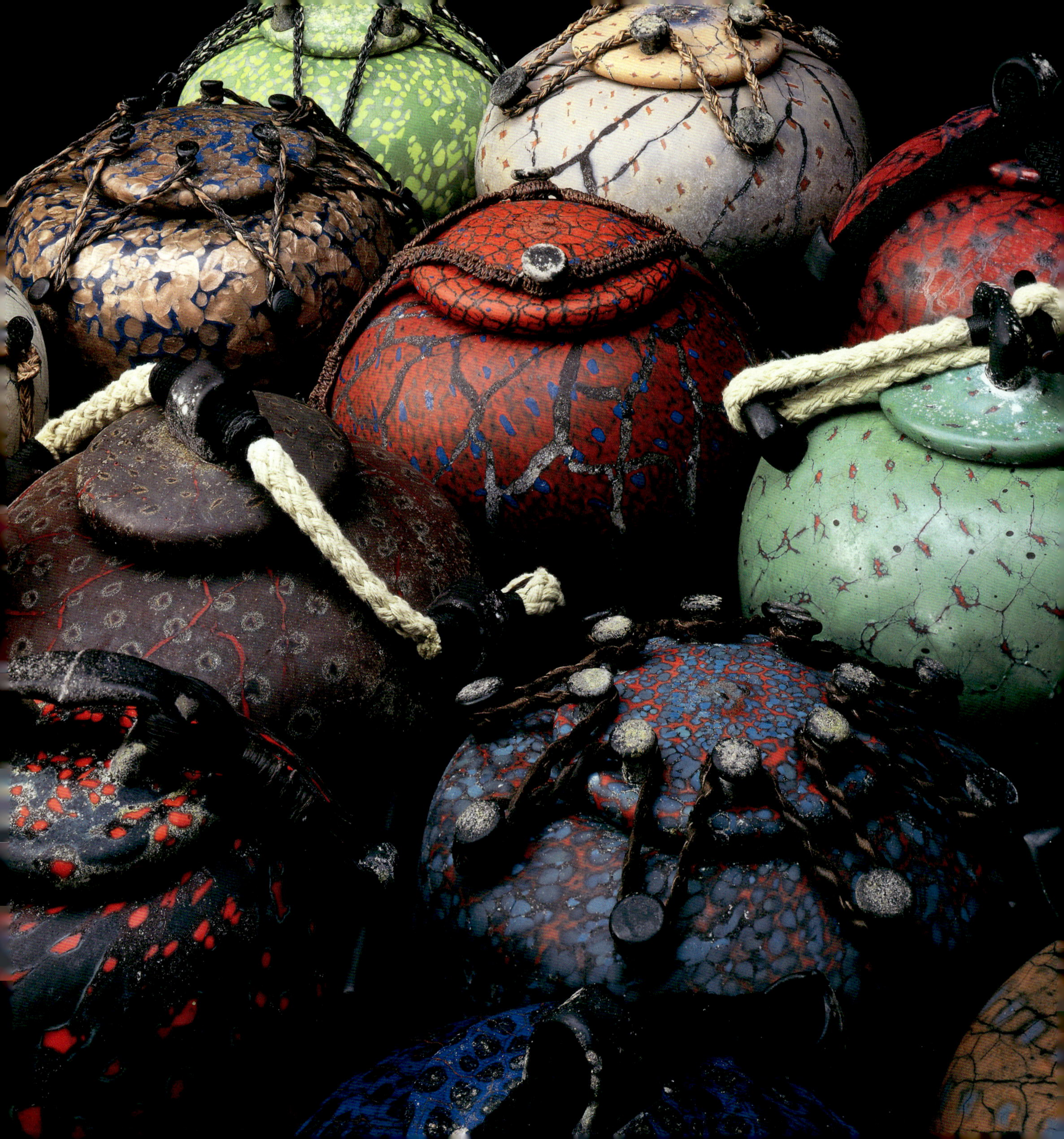

33

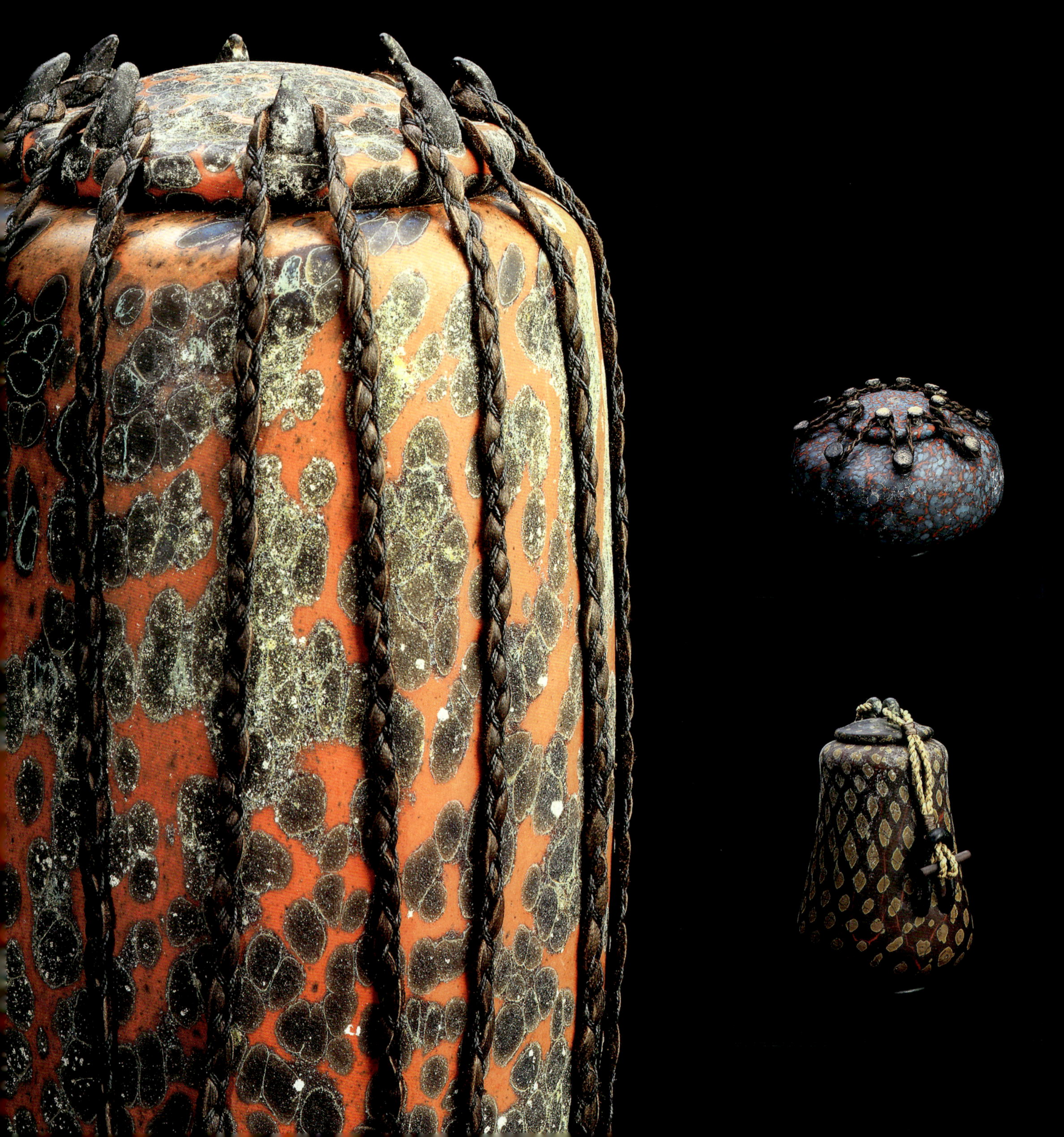

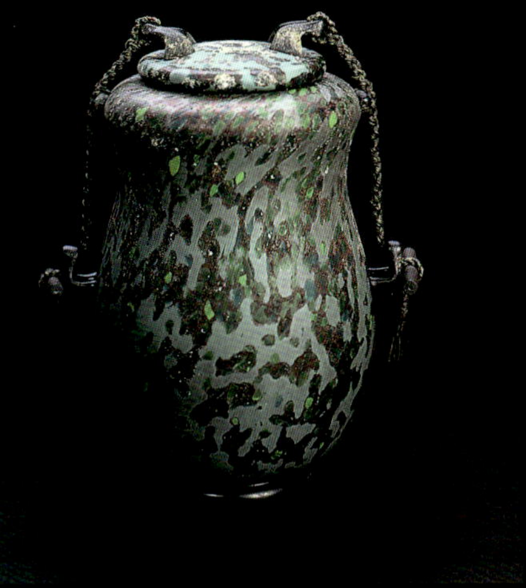
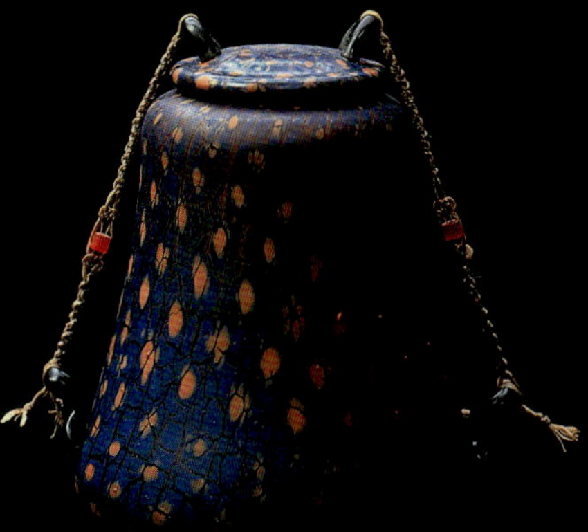
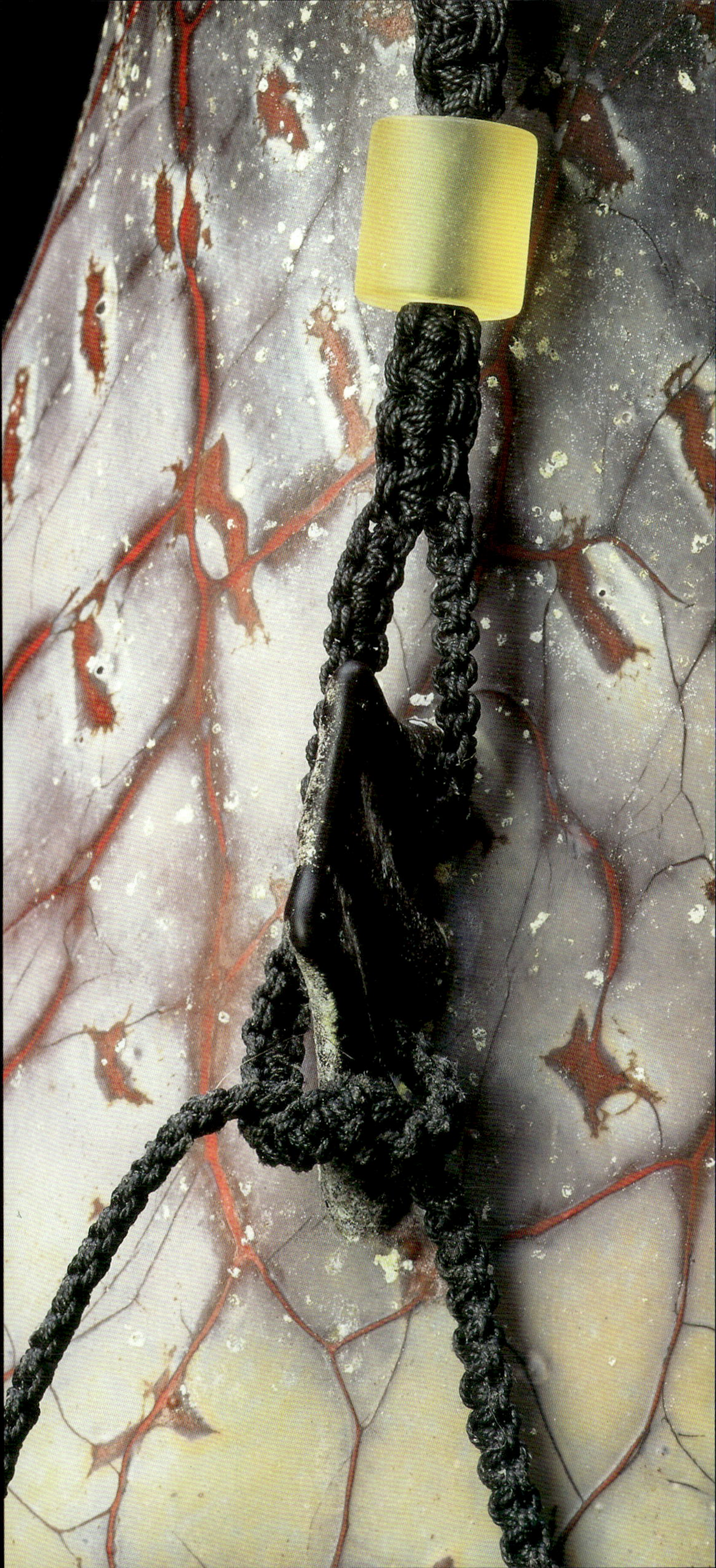

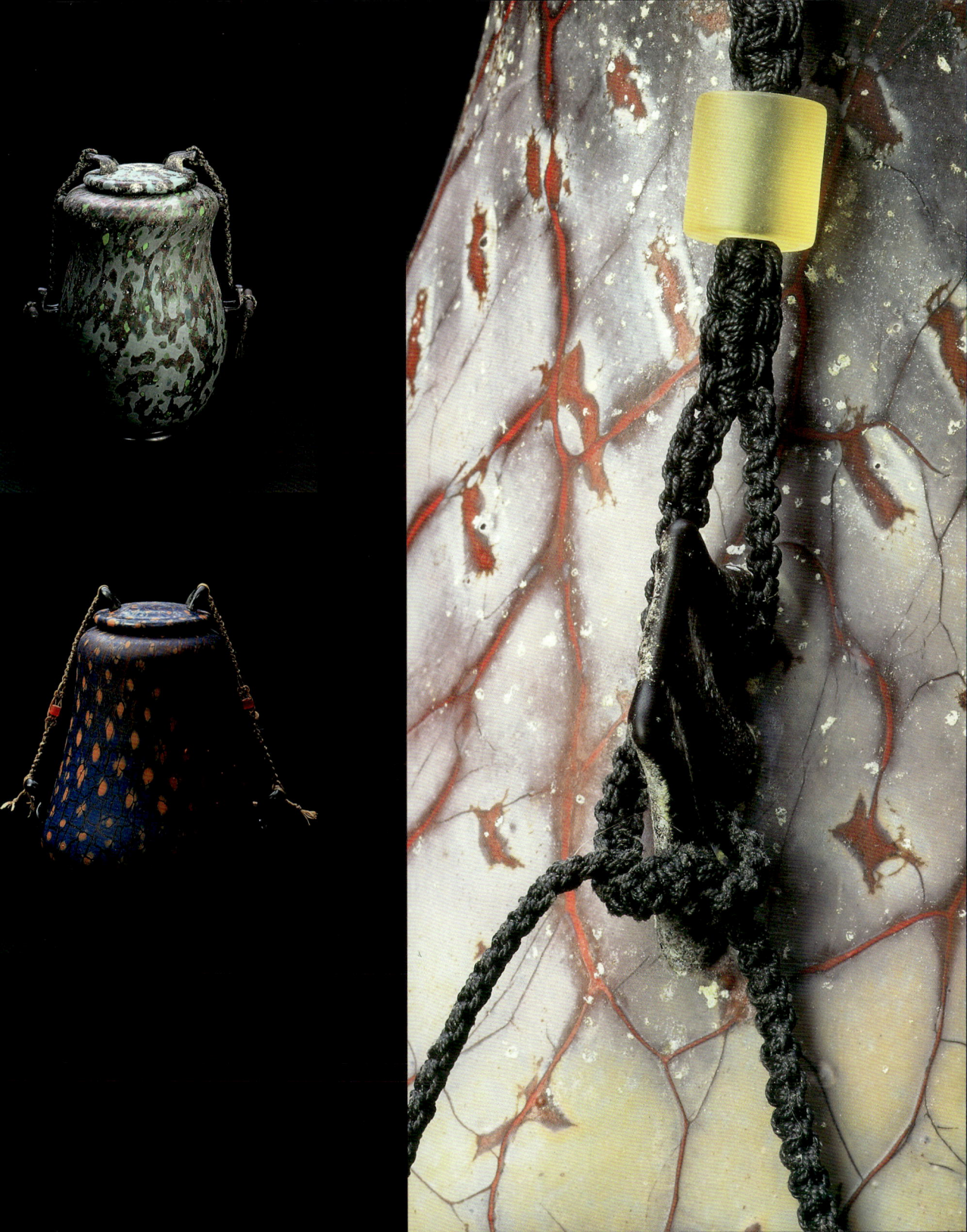

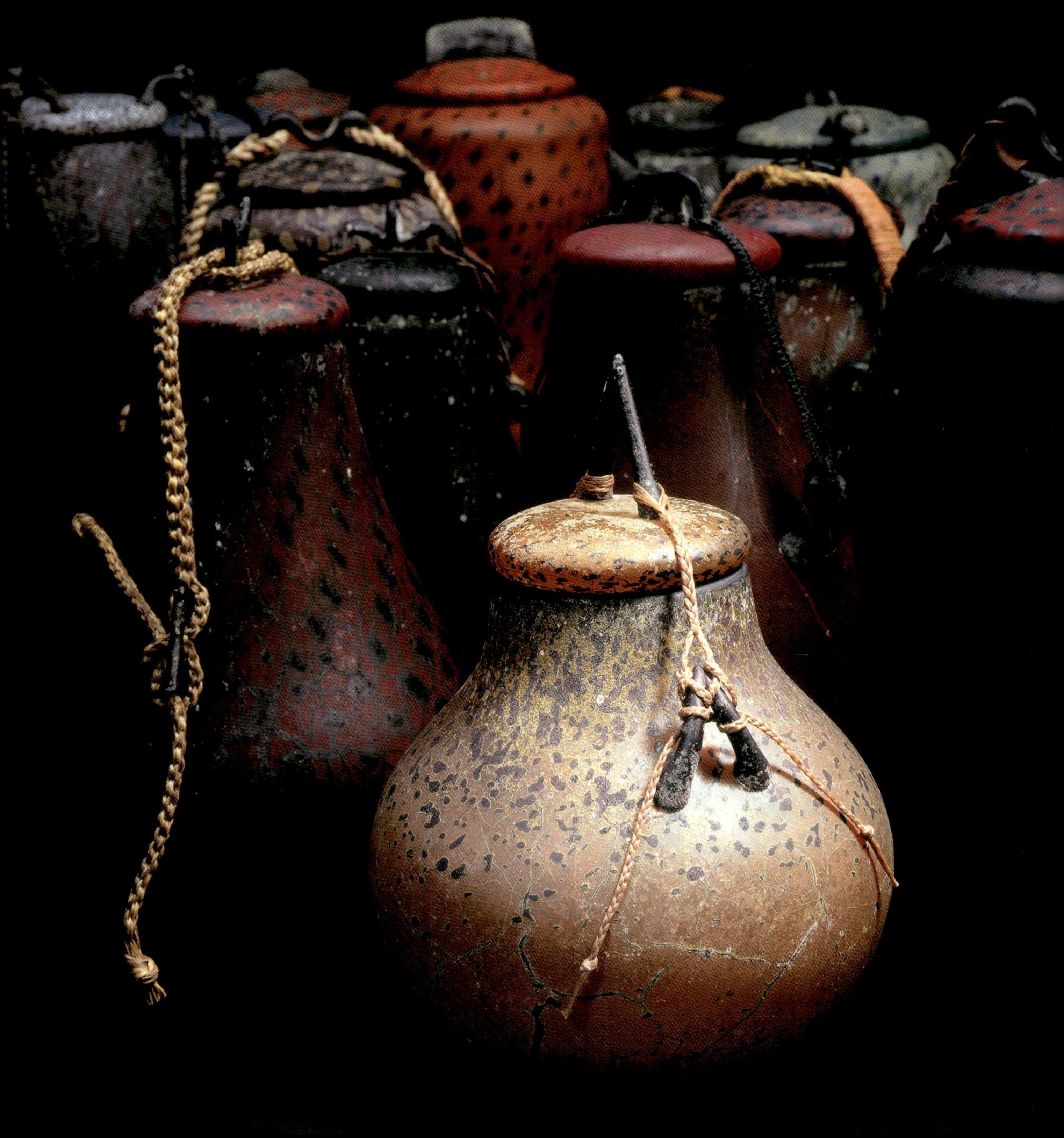

Vessels contain things. And most of the time they do so in a very benign manner, largely indifferent to the various substances that fill them. Fruit or flowers, wine or oil—it matters naught to these mute receptacles that provide those substances shelter. Sometimes, though, a vessel can be inextricably linked to what it carries, its very shape and demeanor an intrinsic part of its meaning—not separate from its contents, but a part of it. Chalices can be like that, and other ceremonial vessels too, but cinerary urns perhaps most of all. These last are the primal vessels, forged for thousands of years of human culture, the hallowed containers in which we place the ashen remains of our loved ones, truly vessels most pure.

William Morris's recent series of cinerary urns echoes his exceptional sensitivity to a kind of transcultural humanity that is both profound and poetic. It is less important to him whether an original historical source be African or Native American, Asian or Semitic. What drives Morris is his vision of the fundamentally parallel human dramas of all cultures, the core tendencies that he sees linking us all in some greater chain of being. We live, we die, we love, we grieve, we wish to have some palpable sense of our journey through this world. Morris's urns are so much more about the living than the dead, our need to honor our loved ones, to take their remains—now somehow purified through fire, somehow both present and absent—and find a vessel for them that has dignity, simplicity, and beauty.

And this Morris superbly provides. The stoneware-like surfaces of these urns (that they are made of glass and not clay is truly incredible, so skilled is Morris's command of his materials) have beautiful repetitive abstract patterns wrought upon them; their lids are secured to the body of the vessels by bits of rope and twine. Cylindrical or bulbous or pear-shaped, these urns are surprisingly subtle in form, each seemingly inevitable, each calling for our respect and admiration. And each is individual, as is, of course, the person whose remains are implied to be secreted within. What William Morris provides in this series is a visionary path for us to reconnect with dignity to an eternal humanity, to sense the profundity embedded in all the processes of life, including the leaving of it.

JAMES YOOD
NORTHWESTERN UNIVERSITY

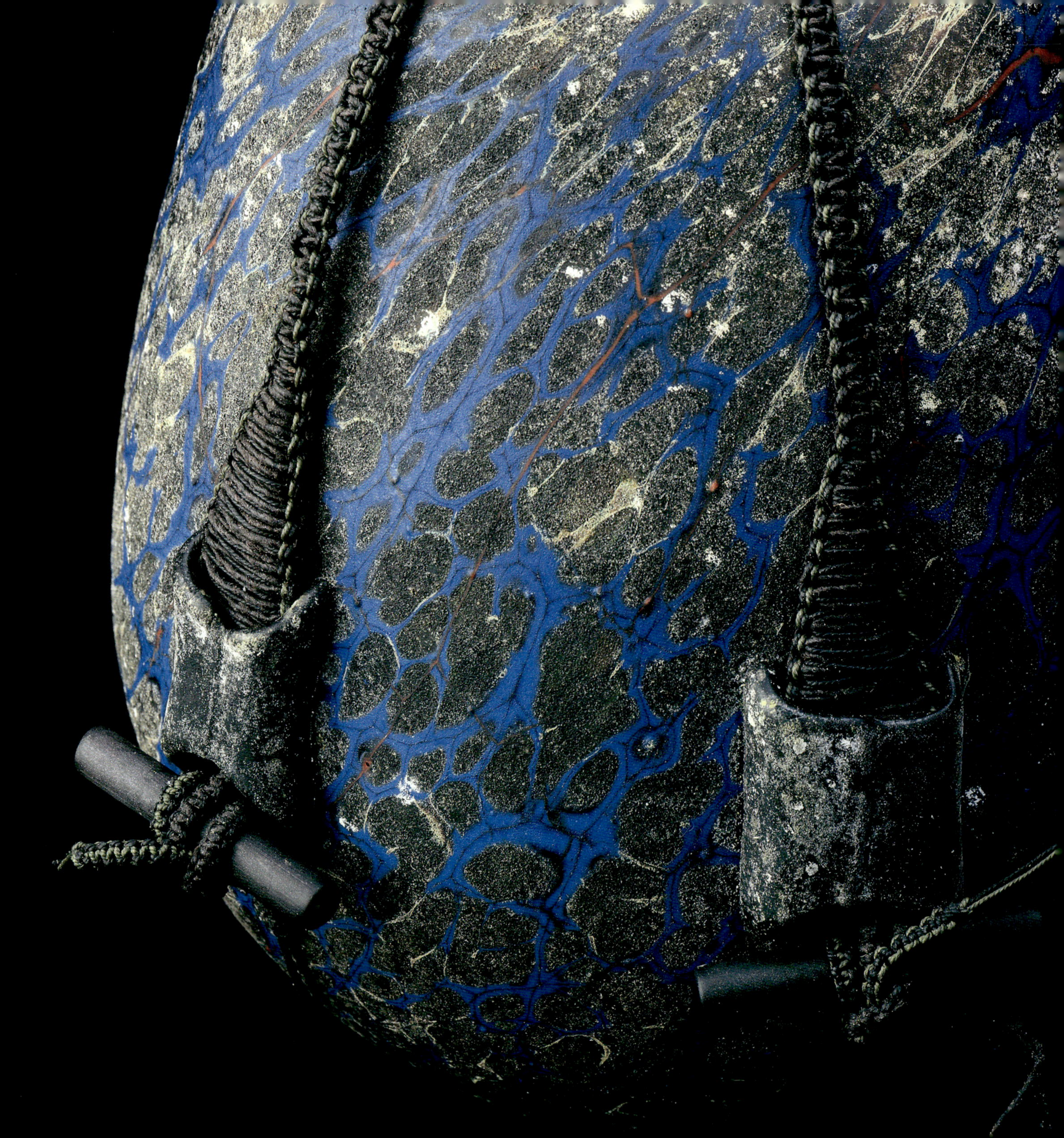

39

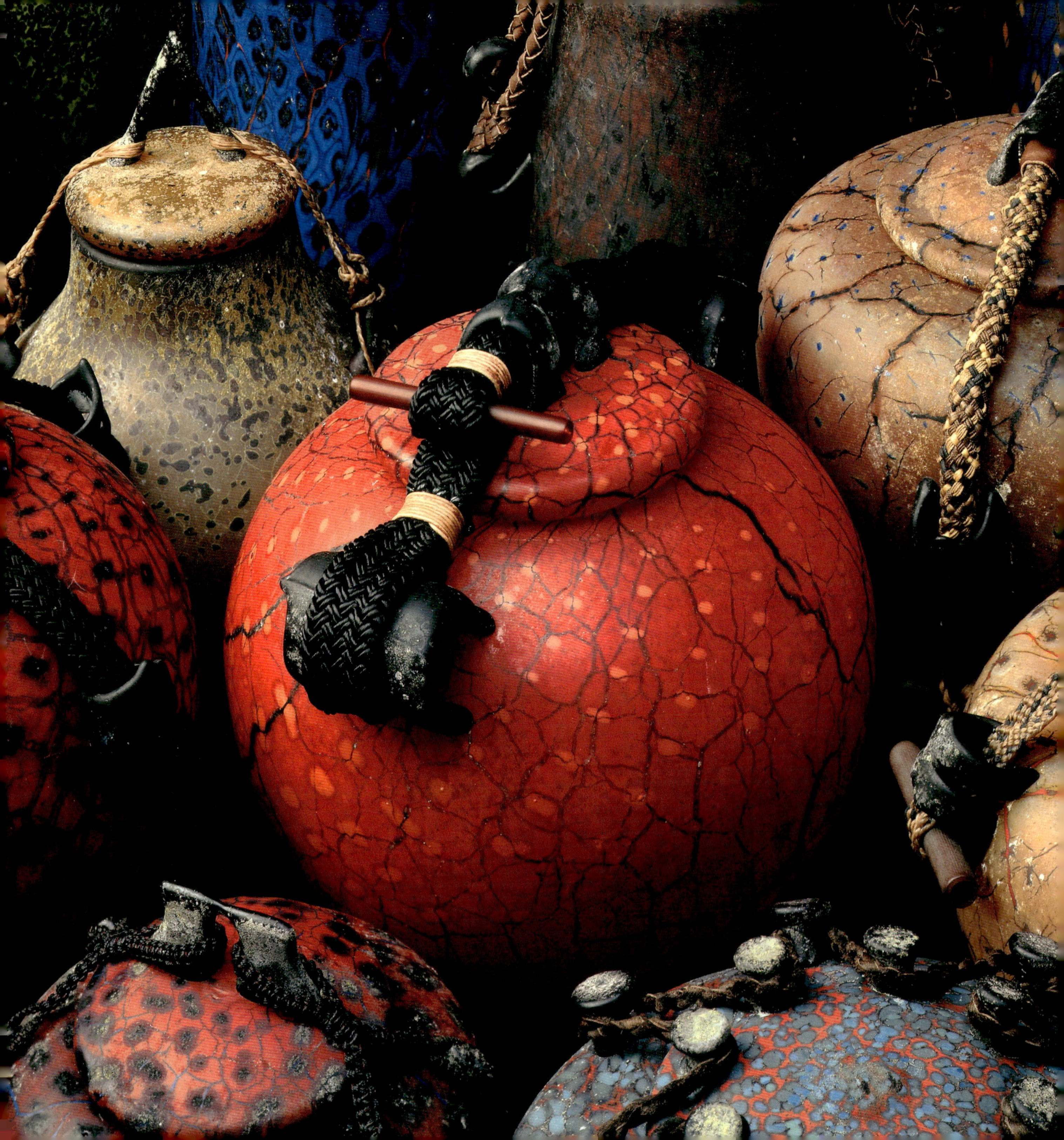

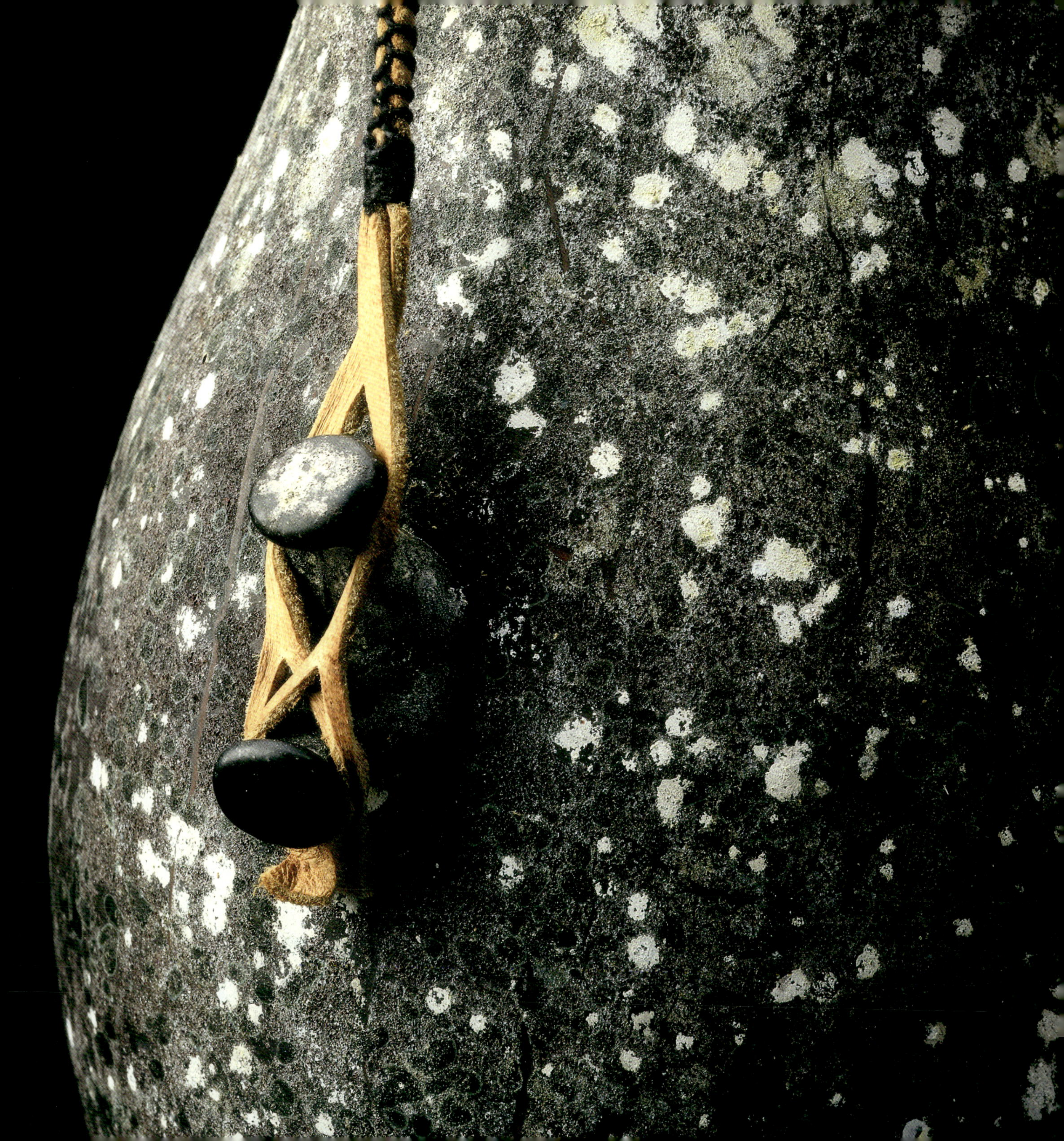

42

43

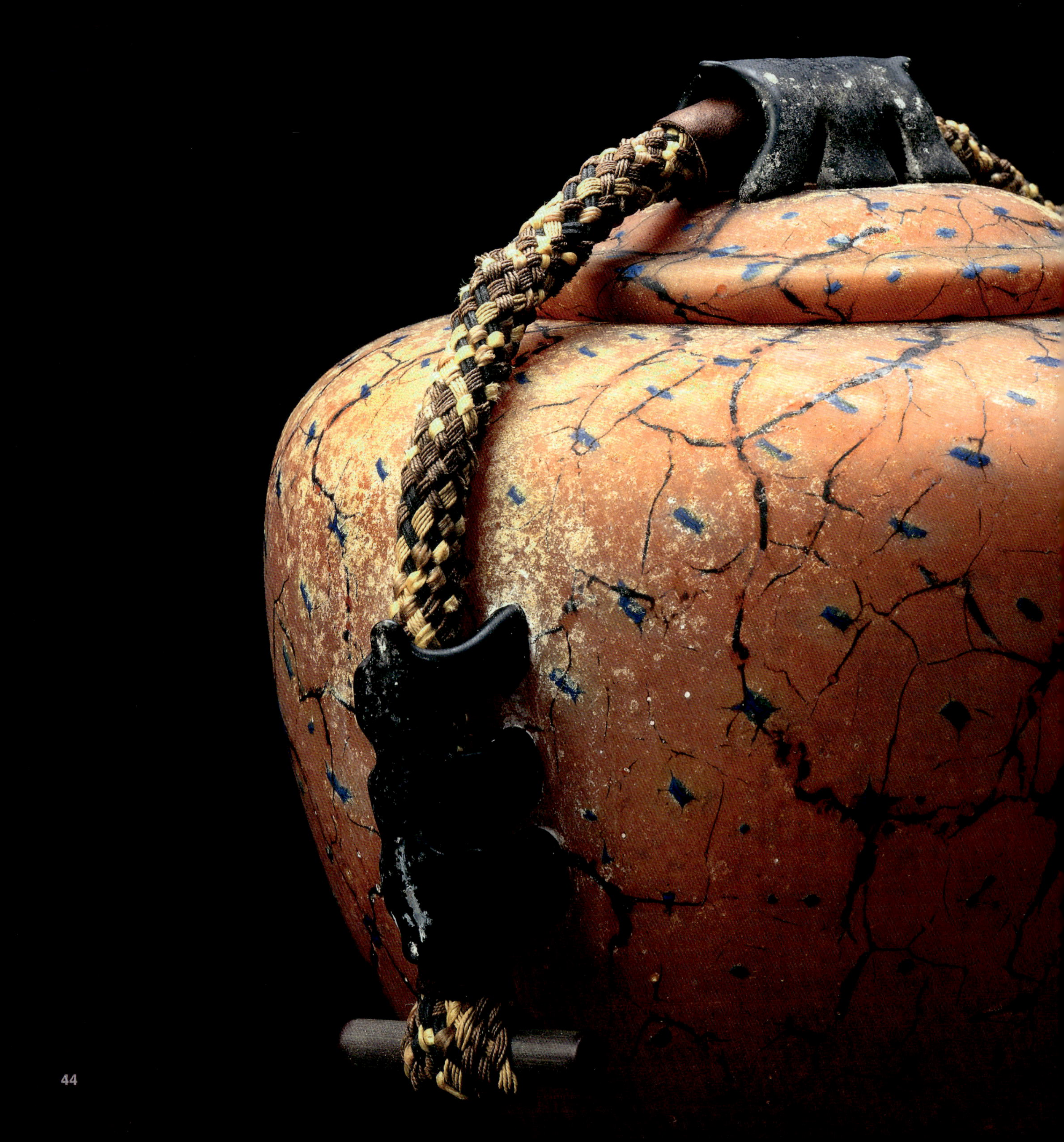

45

Top, left to right: James Hodge, Doug Tillotson, Graham Graham, Trumaine Mason, William Morris

Bottom: Trumaine Mason and William Morris

Top: William Morris
Bottom: Graham Graham
and Trumaine Mason

This catalogue accompanies an exhibition held at the Chrysler Museum of Art, Norfolk, Virginia, June 28–August 18, 2002, and at the American Craft Museum, New York, January 17–June 8, 2003.

ISBN: 0-9706394-1-4
Copyright © 2002 by William Morris
Artwork photography © 2002 Robert Vinnedge
All rights reserved under international copyright conventions. No part of this book may be reproduced or utilized in any form or by any means, electronic or mechanical, including photocopying, recording, or by any information storage and retrieval system, without written permission from the copyright holder.

All artwork by William Morris, except pages 6, 7, and 22: Collaborations by William Morris, Flora Mace, and Joey Kirkpatrick. Fiber closures by Timothy Ringsmuth and Trumaine Mason. All works are blown glass with fiber closures, ranging in height from 8 to 21 inches.

Project Manager: Holle Simmons
Designer: Susan E. Kelly
Copy editor: Marie Weiler
Installation design: Graham Graham
Installation fabrication: James Hodge and Museum Resources
CAD drawings: Jeff Smart
Color separations: iocolor, Seattle
Produced by Marquand Books, Inc., Seattle
    www.marquand.com
Printed and bound by CS Graphics Pte., Ltd., Singapore

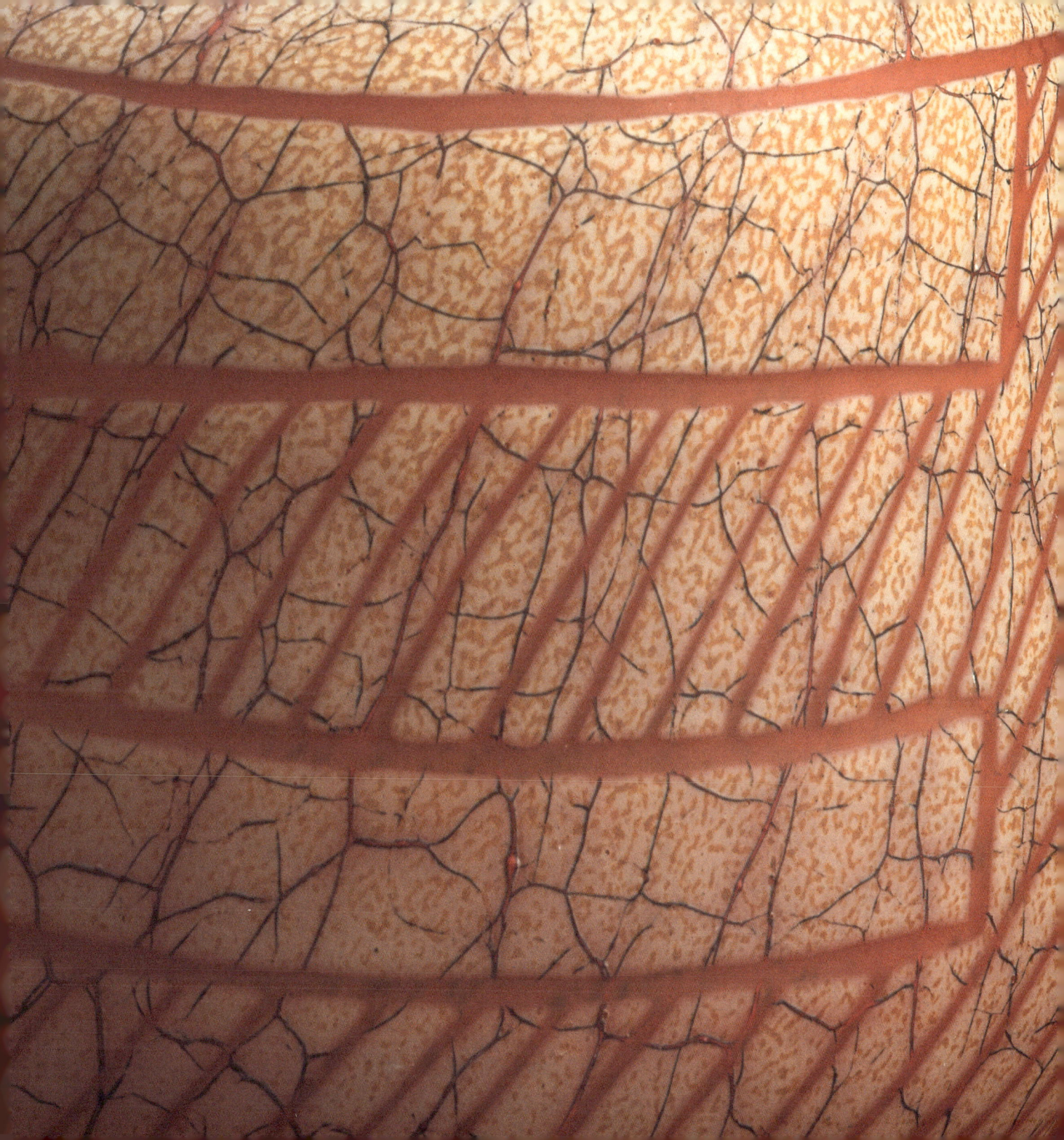